The Maverick

The Maverick

Dispatches from an unrepentant capitalist

by

Luke Johnson

Hh

Harriman House Ltd

3A Penns Road
Petersfield
Hampshire
GU32 2EW

Tel: +44 (0)1730 233870
Fax: +44 (0)1730 233880

Articles first published in The Sunday Telegraph.
Reproduced and first published in book form, with the permission of
The Sunday Telegraph and of Luke Johnson, in Great Britain in 2007.
Copyright © Luke Johnson

The right of Luke Johnson to be identified as Author has been asserted
in accordance with the Copyright, Design and Patents Act 1988.
ISBN 13: 978-1905641-40-6
British Library Cataloguing in Publication Data
A CIP catalogue record for this book can be obtained from the British Library.

Printed and bound in Great Britain by Biddles Ltd, Kings Lynn, Norfolk

Contents

Introduction

Writing a weekly column in a national newspaper is not necessarily a wise career move for someone in business. Managers and investors are mostly suspicious of journalists and the media – with some justification. But I come from a literary family and love constructing an argument on paper. So for roughly eight years I contributed to *The Sunday Telegraph* under the byline 'The Maverick'. The contents of this book are a selection of the best of the hundreds of essays I wrote between 1999 and 2006.

My point of differentiation with other financial reporters was that I actually ran and owned companies – a participant in the process, not simply an observer. So I have first-hand experience of meeting a monthly payroll, backing a business that then goes bust, and the joy that comes when you discover a winning commercial formula. Inevitably I tend to put forward a personal point of view: few of my pieces are balanced. I am the sort who prefers prose without the phrase 'but on the other hand'. But I always believed the opinions I expressed were those of many entrepreneurs, who were perhaps too busy to find a soapbox, or thought debating such matters a waste of time.

A great many writers and commentators in the media are anti-business or left of centre in their political views. This bias arises because writers and journalists tend to come from the arts rather than commercial backgrounds, and are dubious about the profit motive. Others are from academia, a segment of society heavily divorced from the worlds of industry and finance, and which is mostly dependent upon the state for funding. So by putting pen to paper on a weekly basis I helped correct that distortion just a little.

By crafting an article once a week, over time a writer articulates his personal philosophy. Reading these pieces, it is easy to discern some of my core business beliefs:

- the importance of the entrepreneur in making our whole system actually work;

- the importance of studying business history and learning lessons from it;
- the lag effect in economics, and how we ignore it at our peril;
- the need to do your homework when investing.

There are one or two other messages, but you'll have to actually read the book to pick out the other key strands.

Another feature of the book is how certain economic themes became apparent over the period:

- Low interest rates and a torrent of debt and liquidity fuelling an asset boom almost everywhere;
- The remarkable expansion of China and India;
- The growing impact of the online revolution on the economy, and especially on industries like retailing and media;
- The rise and rise of alternative asset classes like private equity, real estate, hedge funds and commodities;
- The relentless growth in government spending and regulation in the UK, and the consequent long term damage to our national competitiveness and standard of living.

The problems facing society are endless, but I happen to believe we have far fewer difficulties across the world than at virtually any other time in human existence. More citizens enjoy a higher standard of living than ever before, and most of us are living freer, healthier, longer lives too. Despite the doomsayers, progress is being achieved on almost every front, thanks to clever people, greater freedom, and technology. Many commentators say this is a result of democracy. I think a much more important instrument of improvement is capitalism.

Ever since I was nineteen and discovered the excitement of running your own enterprise, I have been convinced that it is the greatest tool ever invented for unleashing the creative energies of mankind. So even if you are not running your own business now, perhaps this book will inspire you to take the plunge. Despite the rise of the so-called 'agent nation' – a land of freelancers – fewer than one in ten of us actually work for ourselves. So there is still room to do better.

Events have moved on in the case of some of the pieces collected herein. Where it has been worthwhile I've added a brief follow-up to bring those articles up to date. Of course trade and industry are dynamic activities, there is constant flux in every sector, and most companies experience fortunes which rise and fall regularly. But many of the salient features of success and failure are constant, whatever the era. Unlike newspaper articles, books tend to endure, and that is why I am happy to see this slim volume appear. I hope you enjoy it, and perhaps even take something away after reading it.

1

Entrepreneurs and the Rich

Why Run Your Own Business?

What motivates someone to risk everything to pursue the dream of starting their own business? Why chase this vision when most such companies fail? What extraordinary urge forces entrepreneurs to keep taking the plunge, despite terrible odds? This question of motivation has always fascinated me: like most things in life, there are a number of reasons, some of which I have listed below.

1. The Money
The obvious basic reason why people go into business is to accumulate wealth. From such riches flow material luxuries, freedom and status – all of them desirable goals. But there are plenty of ways to get rich and running your own business is not the most certain or simplest. So money alone is rarely the prime objective. But nevertheless having enough can be important – as in the famous New Yorker cartoon: "The point is to get so much money that money's not the point anymore."

2. To Build Something
Many are born with the innate urge to create something tangible and lasting. While some become architects or artists, others build companies. They know that a business can give life and prosperity to a community, and almost take on an existence of its own, like a living being. Entrepreneurs understand the vital significance of inventing something that can generate employment. No other creative endeavour undertaken by man is of more practical importance than that. They believe in Sir Walter Scott's dictum: "Ambition is the serious business of life."

3. No Choice
Many entrepreneurs find themselves unable to get a job or provide a living for their family except through self-employment. Generations of immigrants have come to Britain and found local jobs scarce: such resourceful individuals have often somehow found the wherewithal to start or buy a business and become their

own boss. For them being an entrepreneur was a question of survival, not a chance to reach for the stars. Yet as a consequence of their boldness, ethnic minorities own a disproportionate percentage of the UK's most successful enterprises. Too many locals are too comfortable to take on the struggle of making something from nothing.

4. By Accident
I think many inventors, scientists, academics and the like never really mean to become entrepreneurs, but they come to it as a way of making their ideas concrete. These types are driven by a belief in their product and an obsession with making it successful, and the determination to do it themselves if no-one else will. They are often highly technical and not very commercial, but they tend to be intelligent, driven and original.

5. By Tradition
Some inherit a family business, and their sense of duty makes them carry it on. They are not perhaps natural entrepreneurs, and may lack a strong desire for riches or power, but believe in their role as someone who nurtures a family heirloom for future generations.

6. The Challenge
Some are driven to take on difficult tasks because an easy life is not for them. They see starting a business as a metaphorical mountain to be climbed – "because it's there." They realise that they only derive satisfaction in life by overcoming problems, thereby gaining a true sense of achievement. They follow General Patton's philosophy: "From here on out, until we win or die in the attempt, we will always be audacious."

7. Power
Many entrepreneurs are megalomaniacs – they love the idea of not just controlling their own destiny, but everyone else's. They like hiring and firing, making people rich and changing the way consumers shop or deciding what they can buy. Like the railroad king Cornelius Vanderbilt once wrote to some ex-partners: "You

have undertaken to cheat me. I won't sue you, for the law is too slow. I'll ruin you."

8. *Ego*

Some have to be the boss to satisfy their vanity. They enjoy possessing things and creating empires in their own image. They would sympathise with US president LBJ's attitude: when he was moving towards the wrong helicopter an officer said to him, "Your helicopter is over there." He replied, "Son, they are all my helicopters."

My view is that for virtually all those who develop their own business, Alistair Cooke's words about Andrew Carnegie apply: "The chase and the kill are as much fun as the prize."

June 2001

Founder's Courage

I have a feeling that the economy is going to provide plenty of challenges to those in business over the next couple of years. Britain has enjoyed pretty friendly conditions in most sectors in recent times, but many indicators now point to a slowdown or even a recession. So to give some inspiration I have compiled a few true stories of courage under adverse circumstances displayed by a number of successful entrepreneurs.

Henry J. Heinz started his first food business in 1869, when he was 25. His initial product was a home-made horseradish sauce based on his mother's recipe. The business was based in Pittsburgh; other condiments were added to the product range until by 1875 Henry employed 150 staff. But a terrible disaster shortly hit the firm: a buyer bought too many cucumbers and the surplus drove the business into bankruptcy.

Undaunted, Henry picked himself up, and within a year he had started another food processing business with two relatives. Not only did this undertaking prosper, but he was able to use its profits to pay off all the creditors from his previous failure. Today the HJ Heinz Company has sales of over $9 billion a year and is one of the largest food firms in the world.

Harland D. Sanders had a tough childhood, going out to work at the age of 12 as a farmhand. He held a series of modest jobs until he opened a service station at the age of 40, and started serving panfried chicken. His "finger-lickin' good" chicken became well-known, but the property burned to the ground when he was 47. He started again and built up a second success, but a new bypass took all the passing traffic away and he was forced to sell out at a knock-down price.

By now 'Colonel' Sanders was 66 years old and broke. But he had his secret chicken recipe, and so he set out to sell the concept of Kentucky Fried Chicken as a franchise. Within four years he had signed up over 400 restaurants and it had become the world's largest take-out chicken business. Despite selling out for just $2 million in 1960, Harland Sanders remained involved with his creation and lived until he was 90.

William C. Durant is an almost forgotten entrepreneur who helped develop the modern car industry. While only 25, this enterprising individual formed a business called The Flint Road Cart Company. By 1908 this had become the General Motors Company through takeovers and start-ups. But Durant was a somewhat reckless fellow and the business became over-borrowed. In 1910 its bankers seized control and Durant was thrown out – at the age of 49.

But the irrepressible Durant did not give up, and a year later he formed the Chevrolet Motor Company in Detroit. Within two years he merged this into General Motors and took back the reins. Eventually, in 1921, Durant had to step down again, aged 59. Yet the enterprise he built grew to become the world's largest automobile maker and one of the largest corporations on earth.

You can probably guess what King Camp Gillette invented. But his eventual success did not come easily. He was 40 years old and working as a travelling salesman when the idea of the disposable safety razor came to him. It was six more years before the American Safety Razor Company was started, and another two until production commenced. That year the business sold just 168 blades, and the long-suffering shareholders of Gillette's business were growing unhappy. But growth in revenues started to gather pace, and within ten years the business was selling seven million blades a year. Gillette is today one of the biggest consumer product companies in the world, thanks to King Camp Gillette's persistence and inventiveness.

A recent, home-grown individual who has shown considerable powers of determination is James Dyson, inventor of the dual cyclone vacuum cleaner. He spent most of the 1980s struggling on a limited budget to develop his revolutionary household appliance – in the process building over 5,000 prototypes. He battled against multinational competitors and sceptical buyers, working for much of the time out of a freezing coach house near Bath. He says in his autobiography, *Against the Odds*, that success as an inventor takes stamina and conviction. Mr Dyson struggled away for ten years and kept control of his idea and his business, and must be a candidate for self-made billionaire status in a few years – something very few have achieved in this country.

I suspect that all of the above entrepreneurs have suffered worse setbacks than most of us will ever encounter, and yet they all eventually achieved great things. The energy and belief of the individual can always overcome external conditions, no matter how bad they might appear. As Charles Luckman said, "Success is that old ABC – ability, breaks and courage." We shall all need our fair share of these for the next few years, as we enter tougher climates, but the survivors will end up stronger than ever.

October 2002

James Dyson has indeed continued to prosper. His business made £103 million profit in 2005, and is now a market leader in Japan and the US.

Getting on the Rich Lists

This is the time of year when all the Rich Lists come out of the counting parlours, and our growing obsession with material wealth comes to the fore. To add yet more stuff to the pile, I have culled various nuggets from two recent works on the subject of just how the rich get that way. An early conclusion is that it is not all as ghastly as Francis Bacon would have us believe, when he said: "The ways to enrich are many, and most of them foul."

The most interesting of the two books is called *The Millionaire Mind*, and is written by Thomas J. Stanley, a professor who specialises in the affluent. His writing is based on studies of those who live in America's most expensive homes. It reveals a number of facts:

- The rich do not get up earlier than other people – they rise on average at the same time as the rest of us;
- They are not especially academically bright – hard work is more important than intellect or qualifications in achieving wealth;
- Frequently they did badly at school – this drove them to try harder;
- They are almost all married, but have low levels of divorce. Divorce ruins more successful people than business failure;
- They tend to marry wives and husbands who support them in their efforts to get ahead and who are interested in accumulating wealth;
- They tend to be frugal and productive but not extravagant – they might almost be called mean;
- A high proportion are outsiders, who work for themselves and did things differently to the crowd – they were not afraid to challenge the status quo.

And on a slightly lighter note:

- They almost never play the Lottery; and
- They tend to play golf.

The second book is called *How to Be a Billionaire*, by Martin S. Fridson, and might be called a textbook for the really ambitious. Mr Fridson, who works at Merrill Lynch, has studied the "proven strategies from the titans of wealth" and tried to identify the common threads. He suggests adopting the following principles:

- Take monumental risks
- Do business in a new way
- Dominate your market
- Consolidate an industry
- Buy low
- Thrive on deals
- Outmanage the competition
- Invest in political influence
- Resist the unions

Among other tactics, he notes the following:

- Rules are breakable
- Copying pays better than innovating
- Hold on to your equity
- Use financial leverage
- Frugality pays
- Enjoy the pursuit
- Develop a thick skin

The first book deals with the rich – the second with the super-rich. To be just rich you do not have to own your own company or take large risks – to become a billionaire you do.

What is interesting is that the process of accumulation of great wealth itself may create more happiness than the fortunes that are achieved. It seems initial accumulators of money get more gratification out of their fortunes than their heirs do. As Lewis Lapham, an expert on the subject of wealth and class, has said:

"New money is more fun to be around ... Old money is niggardly and defensive." It was William K. Vanderbilt who said: "Inherited wealth is a real handicap to happiness. It is as certain a death to ambition as cocaine is to morality." This is perhaps a contradiction of the classic snob's view that Old Money is more respectable and worthy than New Money.

Thanks to changing attitudes to money in this country, there has been a steady trend towards the individual accumulation of considerable wealth and away from corporate and institutional wealth, which is why the ranks of the Rich Lists have swollen. This trend has accelerated with a bull market and the rise of technology millionaires. This is broadly speaking good for the country as a whole, for much of the dynamism and growth of an economy stems from individual entrepreneurs, rather than big corporate efforts.

In neither of the two books mentioned above does greed feature as a key motivator. Perhaps that is because the rich are embarrassed about mentioning such a base desire. Possibly the authors feel that 'covetousness' – as the original one of the seven deadly sins was characterised – is not an attractive trait to copy. But the drive to acquire is what makes the wheels of our economy turn. We need the rich – and not just for the entertainment value of the Rich Lists.

March 2000

50 Reasons To Be An Entrepreneur

I think everyone should become an entrepreneur. Here are just a handful of the reasons:

1. Because building your own company is the best fun you can have with your clothes on;

2. Because it's still the best way to get rich;

3. Because working for yourself is not just about becoming rich – it's also about making things happen and making a difference;

4. Because if you work for yourself you control your destiny;

5. Because jobs for life and final salary pension schemes don't exist any more;

6. Because if you're the boss you make the rules;

7. Because if you build a company and sell it you pay tax at just 10% on the gain;

8. Because thanks to the internet it's never been easier to set up in business;

9. Because as an entrepreneur you get the rewards for your efforts;

10. Because entrepreneurs are the main source of new jobs and growth;

11. Because being an entrepreneur can be a highly creative endeavour;

12. Because entrepreneurs are cool – just look at the success of TV shows like Dragons' Den, The Apprentice, and now Make Me a Million;

13. Because there is no hierarchy in your own firm – anything is possible;

14. Because building a team and developing talent is really satisfying;

15. Because you don't want to wake up one day when you're too old and say, "I wish I had gone for it with that idea I had…";

16. Because the competition out there isn't really that good and you know you can do better;

17. Because there are more entrepreneurs in Thailand per head of population than anywhere else – if they can do it, so can you;

18. Because there are more sources of business funding – debt and equity – than ever before;

19. Because there are more start-up websites, guidebooks, advisors and other forms of help than ever before;

20. Because the worst that can happen is that you waste some time and lose some money – the world is full of nastier things than that, like illness and death;

21 Because nothing beats overcoming the sceptics and making a new venture a roaring success;

22. Because there is never a shortage of good business ideas;

23. Because economics is not a zero sum game – the more entrepreneurs there are, the wealthier society becomes;

24. Because independence and freedom makes people happy;

25. Because you can tell your boss when you walk out that one day you'll buy his or her business;

26. Because you can moonlight to begin with, and leave employment when you're ready;

27. Because you can build a business with your family and work together for a common cause;

28. Because you can explore your dreams in a way that's impossible to do as an employee;

29. Because you only live once – life is not a rehearsal;

30. Because lots of really successful entrepreneurs started with no qualifications or capital and still made it big – so why not you?

31. Because there are more management buy-out opportunities than ever before;

32. Because creating a lasting enterprise is the best form of legacy;

33. Because it means you can provide for your family;

34. Because it allows you to pursue your passion and make money at the same time;

35. Because it gives you a reason to jump out of bed on Monday mornings;

36. Because the inevitable setbacks are all part of the learning experience;

37. Because if you're a capitalist, you make the world go round – without you there would ultimately be no taxes for any public services;

38. Because creating a virtual business from your bedroom is simpler than ever before;

39. Because flexible, innovative and hungry small firms can beat the complacent big boys every time;

40. Because when you meet other entrepreneurs you'll talk to them as equals;

41. Because we speak English – the global language of commerce;

42. Because despite our system's flaws, the law works, the state is basically honest and property rights are respected;

43. Because privatisation, PFI and PPP projects, and contracting out are creating lots of new areas for entrepreneurs within the public sector;

44. Because interest rates and thus financing costs are low – and likely to remain so;

45. Because banks and other funders have more techniques to back small firms than ever before;

46. Because there are more government grants and initiatives like the Loan Guarantee Scheme than ever before;

47. Because life is not about excuses – it's about seizing the day;

48. Because it might be the only way you can create a decent enough pension to retire;

49. Because if you're an entrepreneur you'll be enjoying yourself too much to retire;

50. Because whatever happens, you'll learn more than by doing anything else.

So what the hell are you waiting for?

November 2005

How Tycoons Breed Success

There are those who believe business all comes down to sex. Prominent among such adherents are certain behavioural psychologists who think the principal motivator for entrepreneurs is the achievement of reproductive success. They study the animal kingdom and draw analogies between the activities of the rich and the mating rituals of lesser creatures.

Such research should not be dismissed as farcical, although a hoary old joke might be in order here. It concerns the 70-year-old who had grafted long and hard to become a multi-millionaire. He then promptly married a beautiful 20-year-old. His friend was very impressed and asked how he ensnared such a lovely young wife. "It was easy" said the rogue. "I told her I was 95."

Many scientists believe women are biologically programmed to partner males with resources, just as females do in all species. They argue that men compete for these resources – or material assets – to achieve social dominance and so win the pick of the girls, and possibly, therefore, the healthiest children. Hence billionaires date supermodels and actresses because frequently the least flawed are also the most likely to survive.

Through history the richest and most powerful men have tended to try to obtain not just one woman but as many women and as many offspring as they could afford. The "trophy second wife" syndrome is a modern day aspect of this propensity.

A further example of this trait was a recent survey which shows that top male executives are five times more adulterous than ordinary workers. All this suggests the accumulation of wealth by men is really about impressing potential partners. As Aristotle Onassis said: "If women didn't exist, all the money in the world would have no meaning."

But the breeding behaviour of the rich is more complicated than that. In the past they have frequently practised a form of inbreeding (in order to preserve fortunes) by marrying rich relatives. Both the Rothschild and du Pont families did a certain amount of intermarrying to keep the dynasties intact. Yet frequently such inbreeding is also accompanied by out-breeding in the form of mistresses – possibly in order to insure against the possible genetic complications of intense inbreeding. Harems were another ancient device which only males with considerable resources could support; these days multiple marriages are the equivalent preserve of the rich.

John Paul Getty, who divorced five times, summed up a possible view of marriage from the perspective of the rich by saying: "A lasting relationship with a woman is only possible if you are a business failure."

Conspicuous consumption is another common characteristic of the rich and has a parallel in nature in what is called wasteful sexual signalling. According to the "handicap principle", many male animals squander energy and resources to demonstrate to females that they are so virile that they can afford to waste effort and take unnecessary risks. An example of such behaviour is the male peacock's glorious tail fan display, which is highly visible to predators.

In a similar way, so the environmental behaviourists tell us, successful men splash out on flashy cars, big boats and expensive art because they can afford to. If everyone could do it, they would not bother. Men covet such status symbols because the other fellow does not have them, and so they may attract the attention of the most desirable mate. The premium is designed to impress the opposite sex rather than offer basic value. A recent edition of a New York magazine says that finding true love in a bull market is all about money and apartments – in other words, offering a mate assets and a good habitat.

It is hard not to detect the influence of testosterone in the cut and thrust of takeovers. The thrill of the chase and the glory of the winner could apply equally to business or romantic conquests. It is much simpler to believe in sex drive as an overall subconscious motivator for the rich, than Abraham Maslow's nebulous "self-actualisation" at the top of his hierarchy of human needs.

Most vague, intellectual achievements such as prizes, awards or titles can be explained as decorations designed to impress the opposite sex. But working out the driving force behind today's ambitious female entrepreneurs is not so simple. For the first time in Britain, quite a number of educated women in their 20s and 30s are starting their own companies as a positive choice. They may well be more maternal and nurturing and show off less than their male colleagues.

Whether the rich are a different species from the rest of us is a moot point. But one thing is for sure – the behaviour of men in business is much closer to that of animals than they would like to think.

January 2000

Corporate Executive vs Entrepreneur

Over the decades I've noticed various differences between managers in large organisations, and those who work for themselves. The main cause is what economists call the agency problem: the difficulty of aligning the interests of managers and owners. The success of private equity is at least partly attributable to the straightforward incentive systems they use. Quoted companies and state enterprises find it harder to devise suitable ways to motivate leaders. So managers do not always act entirely in the best interests of shareholders, and entrepreneurs rarely fit in with big company structures.

In a spirit of fun I have listed below a rather exaggerated top 50 checklist of respective priorities for corporate types as opposed to entrepreneurs.

- Huge corner office vs. most practical low cost office
- Unlimited expense account vs minimum spend possible
- First class travel everywhere vs takes the bus if it makes sense
- Bonus related to sales alone vs dividend
- Size for its own sake vs real shareholder value
- Office politics vs meeting the payroll
- Boardroom fine art vs whitewashed walls
- Fountain in the foyer vs turning off the lights in empty rooms
- Management away days vs conversation in the pub
- Juicy service contract vs sink or swim together
- Let's have a meeting about a meeting vs do it now
- Adjusted earnings per share vs actual cash in the bank
- Acquisition spree vs built from scratch
- Membership of the poshest clubs vs 70-hour weeks
- Combined code vs the owner's the boss
- The chauffeur ran late vs first in, last to leave
- Institutional investor presentation vs closing a sale with a customer

- Increasing HQ budgets vs cutting overheads
- Use the grandest headhunters vs promoting from within
- Let's hire management consultants vs let's use common sense
- High level budgets vs signing every cheque
- Boasting about how many employees there are vs boasting about how few there are
- Executive dining room vs local sandwich shop
- Layers of secretaries vs answers own phone
- Attends charitable functions vs gives own money to good causes
- Cares deeply about CV vs doesn't have a CV
- Keen on a peerage vs never been to the House of Lords
- Hierarchical structure vs no structure
- Sense of self-importance vs sense of humour
- Savile Row suits vs doesn't own a suit
- Obsessed with status vs obsessed with cashflow
- Let's do lunch vs no time for lunch
- Takes all the credit vs takes all the profit
- Risk-averse vs opportunistic
- Boardroom power struggles vs they own the company
- Clings to the job at all costs vs welcomes a bidder if the price is right
- Works for salary vs works for capital gain
- Many photo-portraits in annual report vs photocopied annual report
- Uses highly paid PR advisors vs prefers no publicity
- Talks about stakeholders vs talks about shareholders
- Private equity are the enemy vs partners with private equity
- PA does email vs does own email
- Believes in share price vs believes in long-term investment
- Usually nice and charming vs usually tough and demanding
- Eminently employable vs utterly unemployable

- Part of the establishment vs anti-establishment
- Good at office politics vs crap at office politics
- Buys latest management text book vs doesn't like books
- Lots of grand qualifications vs hated school
- Highly clubbable vs not very clubbable

December 2005

Trophy Wives

Mostly this column is about making money by growing a business or through investment activities. But there is another way to get rich – by marrying money. Now quite often women's magazines carry stories titled something like "How To Marry A Millionaire". These features tell women how to win younger, single men who are loaded. But such pieces have a fatal flaw: most of the really rich men are older – and married already. Thus the way for a determined gal to get hold of a moneybags is to become a Trophy Wife.

It should be emphasised up front that becoming a Trophy Wife is no pushover. It takes serious work and continuing application. Men who have made it are by their nature demanding, and have to be sold. Moreover, they are often still married to a first wife, so the applicant Trophy Wife has to deal with her as well. Rich men may well be frustrated and have a loveless marriage – but to dump the wife for a newer model is an expensive and painful process, even for a billionaire. They have to go through the cost and publicity of a divorce. They are only going to do it for someone who really brings a lot to the partnership.

Trophy Wives are important acquisitions for men who have everything. These tycoons have already got the yacht and Gulfstream jet. They frequently marry young and have worked obsessively to amass great fortunes. They have achieved wealth, fame and power, but they no longer find their first wives sexy or sophisticated enough for their newfound status. Perhaps they never had time to sow their wild oats when they were young, since they were too busy empire building. They reach late middle age and they want to relive their youth – roll on the Harley Davidson and leather jacket, turn up the disco music – let's party!

These magnates are rich enough to divorce and are used to getting the best. When they were poor and striving, their wife was supportive and brought their children up, but she was never much of a beauty. A Trophy Wife has to be much younger and prettier than the first, and understand sexual techniques which blow the tycoon's mind (and much else). Trophy Wives are manic about keeping in trim and use personal trainers. They are also more ruthless and less romantic than the wives they replace. They understand their relationship is a bargain whereby they supply sex, glamour and youth, while their new husband supplies jewellery, a large house and endless expensive holidays. Often Trophy Wives are more exotic than the dowdy mothers they supersede – certainly better travelled, and quite possibly foreign.

A Trophy Wife is not usually expected to have children – although she'll often have to cope with resentful children from the first marriage. Rather her tasks will be to add new friends, new clothes, a new home and new interior decoration to her husband's world. She will introduce modern fashion and art to his life, and host exotic parties – she will know how to spend serious money on their fabulous life together. She will fuss about his health and get him on a fitness regime. She understands a lot about her husband's business, probably because she did plenty of homework before she picked her target. Because these Trophy Wives are usually successful career women themselves, they offer a contrast to their husband's first wife, who spent all those years bringing up a family and making sacrifices for her husband's business. The first wife didn't have time to work out or become a high flyer – she was dutifully looking after the children and home.

The bad news for would-be Trophy wives is that their husbands are more often than not boorish, sad figures. They are selfish and terrified of ageing, and have proved how disloyal they are when it comes to their own desires. All would-be Trophy wives need to ensure a favourable pre-nuptial agreement is drawn up to protect them in the event their rich husband wants to make yet another trade for a younger model.

Historically the men who today acquire Trophy Wives had mistresses – pampered younger women spoiled by their rich older lovers. Big businessmen like robber baron Jim Fisk and auto pioneer Henry Ford both had secret lovers. But these days divorce is more socially acceptable and intelligent, ambitious women are not satisfied being a mere courtesan. They insist on being installed as a fully-fledged partner. After all, the rewards can be substantial.

Anna Nicole Smith in Texas was not the classic Trophy Wife, since she lacked serious sophistication. But she did hit the jackpot when she married old J. Howard Marshall. He was 89, wheelchair bound and worth hundreds of millions from oil. She was in her twenties and a dancer and topless model. He died within two years of their wedding – but it took her several more years of litigation before she got her share of the estate. But to suggest her motivation might have been financial, rather than love, is seedy and outrageous. We all know that such romances would have happened even if the men had been paupers! Isn't that right?

December 2000

Billionaire Politicians

So what's a self-made billionaire to do when he's bored with business? Some play with expensive toys, like private jets; others devote themselves to good works and give their fortunes away; and a few have the desire to achieve high office in public life. But the vulgar pursuit of political power seems fraught with danger for the super-rich. They are better advised to stick to safer occupations like making money.

The unluckiest billionaire politician of recent times was Rafik Hariri, the Lebanese construction magnate. From modest beginnings he made a fortune in Saudi Arabia and returned home to lead the rebuilding of Lebanon after the civil war. But even though he was a Muslim – and no longer Prime Minister – as Beirut's most powerful citizen, the Syrians feared him and his allies. So despite his bodyguards and wealth, on St Valentine's Day this year the tycoon was assassinated with a huge bomb. The backlash created by his murder has seen the Syrians depart from Lebanon as a quasi-occupying force, and Hariri's son Saad has been elected as the leader of a so-called martyr faction now in charge of Beirut. Let us hope Saad doesn't suffer the same grim fate as his entrepreneurial father.

Another political billionaire having a bad year is Mikhail Khodorkovsky, the Russian oligarch. He became a billionaire in just three years through a series of suspect state privatisations handled by his bank Menatep in the 1990s. By early last year he was reputed to be Russia's richest man and worth $18 billion, thanks to the massive success of his oil business Yukos. But then his political ambitions came to the fore, and he started funding parties opposed to the Russian President, Vladimir Putin. The authorities felt threatened, and suddenly prosecuted Khodorkovsky and his billionaire business partner Platon Lebedev for fraud and tax evasion. Some say the charges were trumped up: the state prosecutors point to double-dealing by Menatep. They highlighted the sale in 1994 of fertilizer company Apatit, worth hundreds of millions of dollars, to insiders for just $210,000 in cash. And so a fortnight ago in a Moscow court both the accused were found guilty and sentenced to nine years, likely to be served in a penal colony. Quite a meteoric rise and fall for the ruthless Mr Khodorkovsky.

Meanwhile Yukos itself, subject to $18 billion of tax demands from the government, has been dismantled and its core assets sold back to the state at knock-down prices. Khodorkovsky is appealing against the verdict, but most ordinary Russians – who feel the oligarchs stole taxpayer property on a grand scale – support his imprisonment. While ex-KGB men like Putin remain in power in the Kremlin, the Yukos ex-billionaires are likely to stay incarcerated, as a warning to other wealthy men to stay out of Russian politics.

Over in Italy, Silvio Berlusconi is under pressure. The media mogul was elected as Prime Minister in 2001 with a mandate to shake up the economy. But although his own television, property development and publishing interests are mostly flourishing, Italy itself slumped into recession earlier this year. The economy faces very serious structural problems: chronic government deficits; perhaps the lowest birth-rate in the world; over-dependence on vulnerable export sectors like textiles, furniture and white goods; and basket-case large firms like Fiat, Parmalat and Alitalia. And his premiership has been dogged by a series of criminal trials, which he claims are politically motivated: last year he became the first serving Italian PM to face such a prosecution while in office. Already two close aides have been jailed. He clings on to office, but few believe he will stay in power for much longer.

A more successful billionaire Prime Minister is Thaksin Shinawatra of Thailand. An American educated ex-policeman, he started a small pager business in 1987 and rapidly became the richest man in Thailand by his dominance of the local mobile phone industry. He formed the populist Thai Rak Thai party in the 1990s and was elected with a substantial majority in 2001. Since then he has overseen a significant recovery in his country's fortunes following the South-East Asian collapse. Even the disaster of the Tsunami late last year was handled professionally, it seems. In 2004 Thaksin carried out a crackdown on drug dealers which saw several thousand deaths and an international outcry, but was applauded by many Thai citizens. Predictably he is a disciplinarian, and lives by the Police Cadet School motto: "Better to die than live like a loser". Perhaps that could serve as a credo for all billionaire politicians...

June 2005

In May 2006 Silvio Berlusconi resigned as Prime Minister after his coalition was defeated in parliamentary elections. And Thaksin Shinawatra's government was overthrown in a bloodless coup by a military junta in September 2006. It means the era of the billionaire political leader is over for the present.

Paradise Syndrome

I'm told there is a disease called Paradise Syndrome. The symptoms consist of a feeling of dissatisfaction – despite the victim having achieved all their dreams. Presumably those suffering from this terrible complaint think they cannot find any new challenges. They have ascended Maslow's Hierarchy of Human Needs but there are no more mountains to conquer. For some, it seems, even paradise is not enough.

There is no doubt that climbing the ladder of success involves more and more nebulous goals the higher you get. Beyond a certain point the obvious material rewards are uninteresting: it is fame and glory the ambitious seek. These are perhaps the worst drugs of all, far more pernicious than avarice even. As Tacitus said: "Love of fame is the last thing even learned men can bear to be parted from."

In surveys, even go-getters claim that 'true success' is not measured by the accumulation of riches, but by non-financial rewards like a happy family life and lively friendships. Yet many entrepreneurs and strivers are restless individuals and rarely settle for suburban bliss. Next on the agenda, after they've made their stash, comes acclaim from their fellows. This can take the form of a gong perhaps, or publicity for their great achievements. Fundraisers in America know it's much easier to raise donations from philanthropists if you can give them 'naming rights' for whatever worthy undertaking is being financed.

So how do those of means employ their riches to increase their happiness once they've hit the big time?

1. Honours
The thirst for a gong is very strong among certain self-made types. The ambitious aim for a peerage, so they can hang around in the House of Lords and think they're making a difference to society. The others have to make do with lesser ennoblements like an OBE. These days buying a title by making a large donation to a political party is frowned upon, so massive charitable giving has

grown as an alternative technique to a bauble. Only the snobbish and vain strive for such trinkets – so of course there is insatiable demand.

2. Boats
These can be yachts or gin palaces – but the key thing is that they must be Big. Inevitably most are toys for overgrown children who like to show off. Buying them is normally a financial disaster (I speak from experience) and a form of self-inflicted torture. The problems are manifold: weather, seasickness, engines going wrong, mutinous crew and so forth.

3. Country estates
An essential accoutrement for any man of substance – and has been since medieval times. The British specialise in making a pile then gradually losing it by buying and maintaining a pile – the levelling price of gentrification. Scarcity and a traditional belief in bricks and mortar mean few lose money with such follies – but the cost and stress of upkeep has shortened many lives.

4. Shooting
A key leisure activity for all moneybags. Involves killing hundreds of birds that no-one really likes eating any more. Plenty of keen shots are fairly deaf on one side thanks to years of shotgun blasts next to their ear. Seems a high price to pay to imagine you're Clint Eastwood.

5. Domestic servants
Employing people is increasingly a hassle, and since the death of deference, such arrangements don't really work. Going to a home with butlers and cooks feels like walking onto the film set for an Edwardian melodrama. It's far more relaxing to dine out in a decent restaurant.

6. Private jets
The ultimate swanky executive tool. Ludicrously impractical in Britain and guaranteed to evoke resentment and laughter. They tend to use silly airports and are not as safe or as comfortable as bigger planes. A classic case of the very wealthy buying something

because they can – not because the damn things are efficient or convenient.

7. *Old masters*
The hoarding of hugely expensive pictures has been a favourite pastime of plutocrats for centuries. Usually such characters have no taste in art, but simply collect them as trophies to display to visitors. But the burden of insurance and the threat of burglary mean the pleasure is muted at best. Buying joke modern art is an even more foolish waste of money.

8. *Producing films*
Would-be moguls see themselves mixing with Hollywood starlets and backing a hit. Instead they meet con men and lose their shirts. But the glamour of the silver screen is a powerful magnet. If approached, resist at all costs: it will end in embarrassment.

9. *Football clubs*
Extravagant playthings that mostly deliver misery to their owners. I did business with one such fellow, and he told me that buying a club was the worst mistake he had ever made – even more painful than two failed marriages.

It really does seem that all these vanities merely conspire to induce anxiety and a sense of disappointment. Better to give it all away...

February 2004

Inheritance

I wonder if it is a curse to inherit riches. A lot of people probably dream, as they struggle to work every day on a crowded train, of what fun the idle rich must have! To be born with a silver spoon and never have to worry about earning a living! But the most content people I know are those who have found a productive purpose in life, rather than those who spend their time consuming the fruits of their ancestors' efforts. As William Vanderbilt said: "Inherited wealth is a big handicap to happiness. It is as certain death to ambition as cocaine is to morality."

It is a perversity of human nature that many men struggle all their working lives to better themselves, so that their offspring will not suffer want: but by providing their children with too much, they end up spoiling them. Perhaps those who labour to accumulate assets realise that they may destroy their children's lives by showering them with wealth – but they need that excuse to carry on amassing riches. Possibly it eases the guilt they might feel at being so lucky. Or maybe they like the idea of their estate continuing after their death, giving them some sense of immortality. Others like the idea of building a dynasty, or keeping a family enterprise under the same stewardship through the generations. Who knows the bounds of rich men's ambitions?

One of the great burdens suffered by the heirs of great men is that they always live under the shadow of their forefathers. Forever any success they achieve will be put down to the extra start they had in life: they will never be allowed to win on their own merits. Envy and resentment of their inheritance will permit others to denigrate their talents and laugh at their misfortunes. According to society, any progress they make will be through nepotism. So of course plenty of sons choose different careers to their noteworthy fathers to avoid unfortunate comparisons, and escape the family name and reputation.

Another constant worry for those who inherit wealth is the threat of fortune seekers. I suspect the moneyed classes often intermarry because at least they know their spouse is not a gold digger. It's a desperate reason to form a lifelong partnership, but affluent children are often taught to be suspicious of the attention of those who are less well off. Frequently Old Money marries New to preserve a luxurious way of life and grant the nouveau riche some status and perhaps even a title. Such artificial behaviour cannot be much of a recipe for a satisfying life, but those who have inherited grand estates can find their upkeep expensive. As Swanee Hunt said, after inheriting a $2.1 billion Texas oil fortune: "Inherited wealth does more harm than good. It eats away at your self-esteem. More people resent you than admire you. You never know who is approaching you for what agenda."

The British aristocracy have been through their ups and downs but hereditary landowners still comprise around a quarter of the richest people in Britain. When death duties soared to 75% in 1948, it looked as if the wealthy ruling class were doomed. But thanks to a more generous inheritance tax regime in recent years, inflation in the value of property and works of art, and the careful use of trusts and foundations, many great estates have prospered. Primogeniture and the system of entail mean huge portfolios of assets are kept intact and pass from one generation to the next. In the USA, few of the richest people are descendents of true Old Money. Over there self-made men build bigger fortunes, while divorce, a stronger belief in philanthropy and a tougher tax system mean fortunes get dissipated more rapidly. Both Bill Gates and Warren Buffett have pledged to give their billions away rather than corrupt their children with unimaginable sums. Somehow I doubt the richest two Britons would ever make such commitments. I suspect entrepreneurs have less fear of losing it all, and feel they can spend it how they want: those who were given it may feel uncomfortable about giving away a bequest to charity, because they are terrified they don't have what it takes to make money. If we want a true culture of philanthropy in Britain, we need more newly-minted fortunes.

May 2001

Letting Go

There is a phrase which psychiatrists use when counselling the bereaved, or those going through divorce: they talk about the need for 'letting go'. In the same way, founders have to go through profound adjustment when they sell a company which has been built up over many years.

In lots of cases, the business will have meant much more than work and money to them. It will have been a creative endeavour, and much of their ego, status and social life will have been tied up with their firm. Often entrepreneurs – like authors – only have one great achievement in them. They find it impossible to replicate their initial success. Perhaps they got lucky, or perhaps they exhausted themselves doing it. Either way, subsequent efforts never match their first big win. After cashing out, they spend the rest of their career failing to repeat the early victory – and possibly regretting their disposal.

Perhaps the most enlightened capitalists realise their limitations and pursue a different path in life after selling up. They become philanthropists, or hedonists, or spend more time with their families, making up for all the sacrifices it took to accumulate their pile. The less well-adjusted ones drown themselves in expensive alcohol, wondering why they are so unhappy. You can find them in sad places like Jersey, an island full of overfed tax exiles slowly dying of boredom.

Many business builders are restless individuals, who think that cashing out will allow them to relax and enjoy an extended retirement. For most, this is a misguided philosophy. They are driven, alpha types whose very existence has been fuelled by adrenaline. They miss the rush of business, the buzz of success and they thrive on a fear of failure. Without the challenge and high drama of a living, breathing business to run, they lack motivation and energy, and their life has little purpose – as they see it.

Part of the difficulty is that many entrepreneurs are obsessives. It is only through the incredible dedication and focus of a founder that a business defeats the odds and really works. But these personality types are rarely balanced individuals: they often lack hobbies and outside interests, and they have a narrow circle of friends – mostly in their trade. Frequently they are appalling spouses and worse parents. All too often they fail to really prepare for their retirement, and the pastimes they thought they would enjoy seem tame next to the power and glory of winning orders, hiring and firing staff, and being in charge.

For many ambitious men their entire identity revolves around their career achievements: when they are no longer the boss, they feel lost and useless. Rather than a quiet life, such characters need stimulation and proper challenges. Imagination is necessary to keep them from the graveyard or the madhouse. They require proper goals to believe in. They need to build a new home from scratch, or travel to 50 countries, learn a new skill or start a charity. Someone who has invented a new business from scratch is not likely to find golf seven days a week a fulfilling substitute.

Many have slaved for the big payday, imagining it brings instant happiness. A bigger house, a new boat. But there is a palpable anti-climax when the cheque clears. That's when the phone stops ringing – there's no office or factory to turn up to each day. And then the ineluctable truth emerges: the journey is more important than the destination. The real fun was the struggle. When they were just thirty they had the energy and sheer optimism needed to create a new business from the ground up; at fifty-five it's a different proposition. And what's left – the bridge club?

Some have the adaptability to become serial entrepreneurs. They are, perhaps, the lucky ones. They reignite the great chase all over again, with the confidence, funding and experience of a big win. But others vegetate, wondering what went wrong. They realise too late they are incapable of taking a back seat to passively enjoy the rewards of their efforts. They have a work ethic that insists they go out and justify their existence every day. They need a 'vital engagement', and to use their talents – but the system says they should just coast, fade away and spend their gains.

Clever entrepreneurs understand themselves better: they see that a bit of stress is part of their makeup. They are ambitious and competitive, and while they accept their mortality, they do not want to hasten the coming of death. So they strive to the end, always wanting to make a difference, to create something out of nothing, to live the dream.

July 2006

Legacy

I read last week that our Prime Minister's principal obsession these days is with his legacy. I assume he worries about how his career will be treated by future historians, and whether his legislative record will be seen as a lasting success or a failure.

Entrepreneurs are just as concerned as politicians about whether their accomplishments will endure, or if they will just disintegrate while their lives are quickly forgotten. There is a degree of permanence about many vocations which seems absent from the world of commerce. Endeavours from the arts can last many generations: great works by painters, composers, novelists and playwrights frequently outlive their creators. Film stars and singers are recorded for all time. Generals, statesmen and explorers have portraits hung in clubs and statues erected in their honour: but what of the captains of industry?

Some build up business empires so their children can inherit. But these dynasties mostly wither. Animal spirits rarely pass through the genes, and sizeable inheritances so often cause heartache. Wealthy families once sought to preserve their landed estates, which are fairly static collections of assets: but companies are dynamic and evolve, and require intense supervision and commitment. So sometimes the grand mansions remain, but the sources of wealth which paid for them have typically been swept away by the depredations of time.

Genuine inventors often enjoy an immortality that few business magnates ever reach. James Watt and his steam engine, Samuel Morse and his code, and King Camp Gillette and his disposable razor blade are celebrated while richer contemporaries of theirs are not remembered. Investors, managers and merchants might enjoy success in their lives but are not of fascination to later generations.

Developers and builders are breeds whose activities change the landscape, and who leave a physical legacy. All around Britain there are buildings and streets named after those who constructed them – along with the aristocratic landowners who inherited their wealth rather than made it. Curiously, most property players I know focus purely on profit and care little for the structures they commission, which will still be standing long after they're dead.

After all, business is a utilitarian pursuit: if a firm is no longer economically viable, then it gets shut down. It is always shocking to see the sudden demise after the founder's death of an undertaking which has taken decades to build up. Conditions change, the original energy is gone, the products become outdated – and the Grim Reaper of the corporate world appears – the receiver. Value dissipates like melting snow in the hot sun. Assets that were once in the books at millions are sold for scrap. And whatever life there might have been in an enterprise disappears for ever.

There is a powerful entropic tendency in nature which applies equally to capitalism: chaos is the default state, only resisted by strong characters. As Yeats said: "Things fall apart; the centre cannot hold; Mere anarchy is loosed upon the world." Schumpeter's forces of 'creative destruction' ensure that people, property and the other elements of any firm are recycled into new activities. Technology and tastes move on, and ingenious youngsters replace the old brigade the moment the latter stumbles.

Philanthropy is one device available to the rich which allows them to leave an indelible mark – and do some good. So 'naming rights' are a standard part of any museum or gallery pitch when looking for donations for a new wing or a major purchase. Endowments of educational institutions have been a wonderful way through the centuries for the rich to contribute something worthwhile to future generations. Often foundations have different political views to those who established them: think of the politically correct prizes given by the Nobel Committee, funded by the inventor of dynamite; and the left wing bias of the Ford Foundation – created by the arch capitalist billionaire Henry Ford.

In some ways the noblest legacy of any leader is a team trained and inspired by them. Several chief executives I've known have told me their greatest pleasure in work came from encouraging and promoting younger protégés, and seeing them do well. The conclusion must be that since we shall mostly live to be 80 or more, we should all make efforts to hone our mentoring skills, and engage with the rising stars of tomorrow to pass on our collective wisdom in a systematic way. It would be excellent to see an Intergenerational Club formed to mix veteran managers and entrepreneurs with upstarts, providing inspiration to all. Such an exchange of ideas must surely benefit both young and old – and society too.

December 2005

2
Management and Corporate Life

Business Maxims

Not Invented Here Syndrome
A culture that rejects established experience because it wasn't acquired in-house. This inevitably leads to a waste of money and effort and duplication of mistakes. Such an attitude is characteristic of insular, insecure and arrogant institutions. By contrast, well-run firms embrace useful ideas and research from outsiders.

Pareto Principle
The rule that in many markets and companies 80% of sales derive from 20% of customers. The logical consequence of this is that managers should concentrate the vast majority of their energies on their large, more profitable customers – and forget their many, marginally profitable small customers.

Reversion to the Mean
The tendency for returns and margins to gravitate to the average over time. Thus exceptional profits are unlikely to persist in any particular asset class or market over the long run, as more normal conditions of competition come about. So bubbles burst and deals that are too good to be true are shown to be just that.

Parkinson's Law
"Work expands so as to fill the time available for its completion." A crushing verdict on the culture of bureaucracy by C. Northcote Parkinson, based on his experience in the civil service. It arises because "officials want to multiply subordinates, not rivals" and "officials make work for each other". In organisations where no-one is incentivised to maximise productivity or save resources, this is the natural state of affairs.

Principle of OPM
This states that the easiest route to wealth is through the use of 'OPM' or Other People's Money. Hence entrepreneurs borrow from banks to buy companies, and hedge fund managers raise capital to invest and charge commission and a carry. Thanks to the Fed's easy money policies, the world is more awash with OPM

than ever before, so there are plenty of opportunities to leverage up in one way or another.

Occam's Razor

This rule was stated by Isaac Newton thus: "We are to admit to no more causes of natural things than are both true and sufficient to explain their appearances." This might be interpreted as the view that the obvious, simplest explanations for things are usually the best. Hence businesses tend to go wrong because sales are too low or costs too high, and so forth.

The Law of Unintended Consequences

Unforeseen side-effects which arise from well intentioned actions. So managers are paid to grow their companies, but they then carry out acquisitions for their own sake, which do not add value or boost shareholder returns. Or the fact that the onerous Sarbanes-Oxley rules in the US, designed in the wake of Enron to protect against fraud, are encouraging companies to abandon the stock market and go private, thus depriving investors of opportunities altogether.

The Peter Principle

In any hierarchy, every employee tends to rise to his level of incompetence. The theory was invented by Dr Laurence J. Peter to describe human behaviour inside organisations. For example, great sales people are frequently promoted to manager, where they can't use their selling skills, and where they need people management skills – which they often lack.

Gresham's Law

Bad money drives out good. This might be called the 'dumbing down' tendency. It was named after the Tudor financier Sir Thomas Gresham, who noted that a debased currency will replace authentic coin if both are in circulation. In general, it means that cheaper, lower quality goods will supplant higher quality articles unless citizens attach more worth to the latter than the former. Some misguided persons have asserted it applies in the world of television, as regards the popularity of reality shows etc. This suggestion is entirely without merit.

First Law of Holes
When you find yourself in one – stop digging. In other words, if things are going wrong, don't keep doing the same thing. This is clearly not a principle accepted by the EU: their solution to slow growth and high unemployment across the Eurozone is to introduce more regulation, restrict trade – and blame 'unfair competition'.

Amara's Law
This postulates that we tend to overestimate the effect of a new technology in the short term and underestimate its effect in the long term. An example of this in action was the stock market's over-excitement surrounding the internet leading to the dotcom bubble – followed a few years later by the extraordinary growth of online advertising, and rapid decline of old media like tabloid newspapers.

Murphy's Law
If something can go wrong it will. Anyone who's ever opened a restaurant or done up their house knows all about this.

December 2005

Executive Disease

This week it was reported that many MPs need counselling to stop them turning into depressives and loners. According to a certain Dr Chris Manning, many power-driven people had "psycho-toxic" childhoods, which can lead to psychological problems and feelings of isolation. Meanwhile a major article in the *Financial Times* suggested that people who reached the top in business careers had a rate of psychiatric disorders of 49 per cent.

This is very worrying stuff. Does it mean a high proportion of our corporate and political leaders are mentally ill? Judging by many of the decisions they take, a frivolous answer would have to be yes. Surely only manic depressives and psychopaths could behave in the erratic way some of them do. As Henry Brooke Adams says, "Politics, as a practice, whatever its professions, has always been the systematic organisation of hatreds." And many executives see business as a war of attrition. Perhaps it is no surprise that around 33,000 Japanese salarymen kill themselves every year, perhaps driven to suicide by the pressure of corporate infighting.

I have known two highly successful entrepreneurs who committed suicide. Ten years ago I helped buy control of a recruitment business from the founder, who was under stress and wanted to retire in his forties with a considerable cash fortune. Within a few months he was dead – lonely, and in his mind, useless. More recently I was involved with a merger of a service business co-founded by a professional man. He had been recently ousted from the Board by the majority shareholders, after heavy losses. Deeply depressed, feeling rejected and a failure, he threw himself under a train. Such examples show how highly strung, self-critical – and possibly self-destructive – many entrepreneurs can be. I suspect it's much tougher as a self-employed owner of a small business than head of a major undertaking, where there is much more of community.

It could be argued, to paraphrase Strindberg, that companies are madhouses and the wardens are the Boards of Directors and

45

management. Occasionally corporate life feels like that. Putting everything in proportion always helps. Most of us realise that many things in business are "largely absurd, futile and transitory". But bosses tend to believe they are masters of their fate. They think they can control things and build lasting monuments to their own glory. Of course maintaining control in a downturn, when negative outside events predominate, is even harder. Ross Johnson, the high-spending Chief Executive of RJR Nabisco, had no difficulties putting things into perspective. When asked to justify the hugely lavish fleet of corporate jets owned by the corporation, his response was philosophical: "It's all lost in the sands of time."

The workplace is the last bastion of secrecy when it comes to mental health problems, for the symptoms are invisible and subjective. Indeed, according to a Harvard Medical School psychologist, "Depression is perceived as a threat to your potency – a character weakness." So few in the top ranks of corporations are willing to admit to problems or ask for help. And most corporate leaders are men – who are much less likely to seek advice than women. Yet studies suggest it is the leading source of worker disability and absenteeism. Some believe it is the major killer of people and productivity in industry. In the US its overall cost in terms of lost productivity and medial expenses is put at $70 billion a year.

How does business cope with the rise of psychiatric illness? Firstly by accepting that it is a serious disease. Secondly by realising it is treatable – successfully in three out of four cases. Interestingly the companies that put most effort into offering employee support to those with depression are drug firms – who ought to know what they are on about. They realise it is caused by a confluence of genetics, environment and biochemistry, and that telling staff to "pull themselves together" doesn't really work.

Cures for clinical depression range from serotonin uptake inhibitors like Prozac, to counselling, to transcendental meditation. Employers can help by allowing staff to get their work-life balance right, avoiding office politics and removing the stigma attached to the complaint. Melancholia and anxiety have existed for centuries, and possibly the finest treatments are as old: vigorous exercise and laughter. It's difficult to make out a formal prescription for either of these remedies, but a corporate strategy of encouraging plenty of each would probably do most firms a power of good.

November 2001

Business Language

Anti-capitalists complain about the harm industry does to the environment – but what about the damage management speak does to our language? Admittedly, every profession needs its lexicon. For example, medicine and law have extensive terminologies to define precise meanings. Perhaps in part the doctors and lawyers invented these words for the insiders to keep their world secret from the rest of us. But mostly it was a necessary shorthand that furnished exactitude. Yet business communication really does have too much jargon and obfuscation. Such vocabulary betrays a lack of clarity and lazy thinking. What do the following actually mean: 'granular'; 'traction'; 'reengineer'; 'thoughtware'; 'matrix'; 'paradigm'; 'offline'; 'disintermediate'; 'scalability'; 'bandwidth'? And what about all the hundreds of acronyms: ARPU, FMCG, WAP, EPOS and so on.

Why invent and use such waffle? Partly it lets managers feel expert. Partly it's sheer pretension. And partly it's a weak attempt at being fashion conscious. Ultimately it betrays a lack of imagination among those who employ such gibberish – and perhaps even a degree of illiteracy. Much of this type of verbiage is promoted by consultants and technicians. They are in the game of spin: if they used short sentences and simple words they might get found out, so they resort to euphemism and humbug as a disguise.

Other guilty adopters of business gobbledygook are salesmen and PR agents. Too often they conceal rather than illuminate in their messages, in order to disguise bad news. And they frequently lack the honesty and wisdom to get to the point in a clear way: instead they create a fog of junk English to obscure the facts. This doesn't just apply to adverts or press releases – it can extend to annual reports and presentations. Hype becomes the norm, so that exaggeration is standard and lying acceptable. Today's marketing industries sometimes sound as if they use the Newspeak of George Orwell's *1984*.

Email has degraded the quality of communication badly. Where possible, phone calls are better – personal conversations are best. After all, so much meaning is provided by non-verbal clues like body language and facial expression. Endless documents and conferences have greatly increased the volume of executive guff produced by large organizations. Speechmakers can get away with dull rubbish because there is so much tired information being recycled, and not many of the audience are paying attention anyway. Authenticity, genuine passion and originality are more important in any delivery than appearing slick.

Using fresh, vigorous language in the spoken and written form is not easy and takes practice. Executives don't have to be masters of English Literature. But when you can read dozens of job adverts every week in *The Guardian* for public sector posts and it's unclear what any of the applicants are meant to do as work – then you see the dangers of sloppy language. Executives need to be constantly on the lookout for cant, because it probably indicates chicanery. As Ecclesiasticus said: "Let thy speech be short, comprehending much in a few words." After all, the really significant insights are rare and generally take little explaining.

Certain departments within organisations produce more than their fair share of incomprehensible words and phrases. The IT specialists are the worst, closely followed by the marketing division and the personnel people. Using code is a way for them to take their careers more seriously and get an edge over other departments. Sadly, these developments are not new: ever since the profession of management was invented in the 1950s, there has been more and more jargon.

To combat the slew of ambiguous and phoney language from the boardroom, some clever people have written a special computer programme which detects dodgy usage, called 'Bullfighter'. It's free on www.fightthebull.com There's a book too, called *Why Business People Speak Like Idiots*. But neither beats the best antidote to the bull****: reading great books by outstanding writers, all the while learning how compelling sentences and paragraphs are constructed.

Some linguists argue that English constantly evolves, and that new technical phrases are part of that process. I accept that our language isn't static, and indeed one of the joys of our mother tongue is the way it absorbs useful words from other languages. But in prose and oration there is no excuse for over-complex and confusing words and structures. If you want to really make an impact, then discard bland clichés, cast aside the pedantic and the opaque – and stick to plain English.

November 2005

Seven Deadly Sins

A rational observer might suspect that the laws of applied economics are behind all the striving that characterises the world of commerce. But it could be that a more ancient set of principles controls the invisible hand of trade: I refer to The Seven Deadly Sins. After all, St Paul states in 1 Timothy (6,10): "For the love of money is the root of all evil." Is this really true?

First of the sins in business must be *pride*. St Thomas Aquinas thought so: "Pride, which is the desire to excel, is said to be the beginning of every sin." Who has ever met a chief executive without ego and conceit? Arrogance and ambition are more common in boardrooms than tables and chairs. Humble, self-deprecating bosses are as rare as profit upgrades these days. Perhaps it is inevitable that a successful company owner should be proud of his creation. But is this a morally good thing? That is a difficult question to answer.

The other outstanding capitalist sin is covetousness – or *greed*. The desire for material things is a universal trait among the executive classes: bigger homes, second homes, grander limousines, boats, fine antiques and so forth. Ours is an age of possessions – ever more luxury goods, whole generations engaged in the endless pursuit of getting and spending. Curiously, even in ancient times philosophers knew that expensive acquisitions do not tend to result in happiness. Rather, contentment arises from intangibles that cost nothing, such as laughter, friendship and love. It seems retail therapy is hogwash.

Envy is rampant in modern life, but it was probably always so. In business this unattractive failing is often called 'being highly competitive'. It can certainly act as a spur to effort, but often it leads to hate and destruction. Obsessive scrutiny of rich lists is the mark of an envious type. I know one high achiever who writes to the compilers of such studies to point out that they have underestimated his wealth. What is really surprising is that he feels no shame or guilt in telling anyone who cares to listen that he has done so! Of course envy tends to make those who suffer it deeply unhappy. Gregory the Great said of the envious man that "the self-inflicted pain wounds the pining spirit, which is racked by the prosperity of another."

Gluttony is visible everywhere these days: we have become too good at producing and selling food, and the growing ranks of the obese testify to our poor self-discipline. Interestingly, in surveys among American women, their single greatest desire in life is not to be rich or famous – but to lose weight. The spirit is willing but the flesh is weak.

Business is also brilliant at tempting *lustful* desires in us: everyone knows sex sells like nothing else. My observations also lead me to believe many top entrepreneurs succumb to lustful urges rather more than most – perhaps contributing to the high incidence of broken marriages among the very wealthy.

Many businessmen suffer from anger or *wrath*. I've attended plenty of boardroom bust-ups over the years. Most revolve around other sins like pride or avarice. I've found anger to be at least as damaging a sin as any of the others – both to those who lose their temper and to those who suffer the outburst. Again I think many bosses have a bad temper because they are powerful enough to get away with it, just as the rich can be more gluttonous because they can afford to eat so much.

Sloth is hardly a characteristic of most go-getting capitalists. As a society we do less physical work than we used to and take more holidays, but laziness is surely not common among successful managers. Indeed, it is perhaps the worst sin in the eyes of the business community: high flyers are always expected to be rushed off their feet.

As a counterbalance, Plato proposed four cardinal virtues: justice, prudence, fortitude and temperance. They are in short supply in the executive suite. There is little justice in the dog-eat-dog world of business, otherwise monsters like Robert Maxwell would never have risen to the top of the heap. Prudence is not a trait much admired among bulls in the market – they see themselves as dedicated risk-takers. Fortitude – courage in the face of adversity – is perhaps seen as a virtue in the world of commerce. Temperance? Well, when was the last time you saw an entirely sober office celebration of any kind?

So does this quick theological analysis mean you have to be evil to get ahead in business? Well, no – most Chief Executives I've met are decent, moral individuals. But I have a suspicion that a few might have sold their souls to the devil. Just take care when you're dealing with them...

January 2002

Corporate Comedy

Corporate executives are usually portrayed as humourless drones, but the truth is they enjoy a laugh like everyone else. After all, the best selling series of business books of all time are the Dilbert cartoon strips – which suggests there is a need for more fresh jokes in the boardroom – and I don't mean clowns pretending to be non-executive Directors.

So far this year I've come across three great pieces of business comedy. The first is a combined book and website called f**kedcompany.com. It is a graveyard analysis of doomed internet companies. For anyone who had an involvement with the dotcom bubble, it is a painful journey. I made my fair share of – with hindsight – ridiculous mistakes. Reading about the waste, greed and stupidity of hundreds of start up disasters is educational – and hilarious. It is a reminder that for a brief period in the late 1990s there was a complete suspension of disbelief and a terrifying optimism abroad in the commercial world – the like of which we may never see again. The losses may pale into comparison beside the telecom industry collapses – but My God! were we over-confident and deluded...

Whole mini-sectors came and went within the blink of an eye, having lost fortunes. Pets.com, Petstore.com, and Petopia.com tried to sell pet food over the net. They raised around $300 million between them and all shut down or were sold for peanuts. Kozmo.com and UrbanFetch.com delivered videos ordered over the web. They blew another $300 million between them – and even had investors like Amazon.com and Starbucks among the losers.

Some concepts were so foolish they make one weep. Furniture.com spent $2.5 million on their domain name alone, and then discovered shipping costs were too high for the business to have any economic sense. One ex Furniture.com engineer said, "There were many cases when we would get an order for a $200 end table and then spend $300 to ship it." No doubt they thought they would make it up on volume.

In almost every case companies spent far, far too much on over-elaborate websites and flashy advertising and failed to get the logistics right. Investors and entrepreneurs refused to believe that customers mostly use the net to research and compare – but not necessarily to buy. Mad projections and nonsensical market statistics combined with technology mumbo-jumbo to produce the most outrageous destruction of value since the sacking of Rome. An extension of the original concept is www.internalmemo.com, an anarchist collection of corporate emails. They are mostly self-congratulatory rubbish from ailing organisations like WorldCom, and make quite amusing reading.

My favourite live business spoof of the year is 'L. Vaughan Spencer', a take-off 'gangsta motivator' speaker I saw perform at the Edinburgh Fringe. His motto is "Don't Be Needy Be Succeedy" and he has his own website, www.thesucceeder.com. He styles himself as a 'personal growth guru' and is the perfect antidote to the endless bogus management consultants and coaches who ply the corporate circuit. He talks more sense than most authors of management books – even though it's all a spoof. L. Vaughan (who is really comedian Neil Mullarkey) is doing a show on October 17th at The Brighton Comedy Festival – catch him if you can.

The third source of business laughs is www.satirewire.com, a site that invents fake financial and political news stories. Items include headlines such as "Investors Stunned to Learn Cisco Not Just Stock, Also Company That Makes Things – Betrayed shareholders not particularly interested in routers, switches" and "Enron Admits It's Really Argentina – Now massive ineptitude, corruption make more sense, analysts say". Andrew Marlatt, who runs the site has written a book, *Economy of Errors*, that features most of the best phoney stories. I like one that discusses a $100 billion IMF country loan to fund "civic infrastructure improvements". The IMF spokesperson explains, "That usually means the president is going to build a palace."

The new generation of business humour is more vicious and

specific than the rather gentle classics like *Parkinson's Law* or The *Peter Principle*. Such a shift is a reflection of changing tastes, and the extreme and uncertain times in which we live. At least we haven't forgotten how to have a laugh – even at work.

September 2002

Vicious Business

There are boatloads of tedious management books published every year, mostly written by nonentity gurus who have never done much, except give dull lectures. I find these sort of books ideal for inducing sleep, but neither entertaining nor instructive in a practical sense. However, I have just come across one of the more unpleasant management books recently published, and a jolly good read it is too. It's called *Eat or Be Eaten* – the author, a certain Phil Porter, must be a complete monster to work with.

The entire premise of the book is that business is unrelenting jungle warfare – and most of the enemies are your work colleagues – not the competition. It is all about how to get people fired, demoted or demoralised, and how a Master Corporate Politician can conquer any possible rival, if they are willing to be devious and ruthless enough.

It is a sort of reworking of *The Prince*, by Machiavelli, surely the first management book of all time. Originally published in 1532, this work has been held as inspiration for generations of dictators and tyrants who have used whatever means are necessary to seize and hold power. Some argue that Niccolo Machiavelli has had a poor press: don't you believe them. I give you two examples of stratagems from his blood-chilling manual.

He describes how certain citizens have become princes through "villainy and infinite treachery". These types are recommended to undertake "well committed cruelties" – vast massacres of their enemies all at once, rather than dithering around with sporadic executions – if they want to retain power. It brings to mind Stalin's chilling remark: "A single death is a tragedy; a million deaths is a statistic."

As a for instance, when Cesare Borgia took the Romagna in Renaissance Italy, he deliberately put in charge Messer Remirro de Orco, who was exceedingly cruel to the newly-conquered citizens. Once the locals had been subdued, in order to be liked, Borgia himself then found an excuse to dismiss his minister and had him cut in half and placed one morning in the public square at Cesena with a piece of wood and blood-stained knife by his side. Machiavelli then says: "I feel bound to hold him up as an example to be imitated by all who by fortune and with the arms of others have risen to power."

Another modern day treatise on seizing power is *What Would Machiavelli Do?* subtitled 'The Ends Justify The Meanness' – by Stanley Bing, a brilliant columnist with *Fortune* magazine. Although it is a spoof book, I think the author is sincere in much of what he says, which is essentially that nasty people win. It is a depressing conclusion if it is right. The entire volume is about how to shaft everyone, behave in a generally malevolent way and get to the top of the heap. Virtue and decency are seen as vulnerabilities.

I admit I am a bit concerned about the ethics of these books. It seems the writers all feel that morals just clutter the corporate landscape – the issue is about taking power and money, and keeping it – and tough if people get hurt on the way. Of course the two modern texts are by Americans, and inevitably all three are by men. Women are less concerned about materialism, status and dominating other people, whereas ambitious men only really care about their achievements and winning. (One honourable exception is Linda Wachner, the awful sounding President, CEO, and Chairman of Warnaco Inc., who memorably shouted at senior executives: "You're eunuchs. How can your wives stand you? You've got nothing between your legs.")

Do I really think many business leaders would secretly agree with the principles put forward in these sinister manuals? Is politics in business truly so horrible that only sons of bitches make it, and then by trampling over lots of bodies? These studies suggest that Richard Crossman's views on power were accurate: "Slavery of the acquiescent majority to the ruthless few is the hereditary state of mankind." One can imagine plenty of megalomaniac entrepreneurs agreeing with all this.

The misdeeds proposed in these books are legion: Do not

hesitate to lie when necessary; Carry grudges; Be happy to make enemies if necessary – as long as you can defeat them; See business as a continuous war, with no rest; Focus obsessively on the money; Punish mistakes ruthlessly; Take advantage of others' weaknesses; Keep subordinates in a permanent state of fear; Have no patience; Suffer no self-doubt or conscience whatsoever; and so on. On thinking about it, I definitely have met a few characters who have been using *The Prince* as a textbook.

I suppose little has changed since the 15th century, when an exiled Florentine nobleman sat down to write *The Prince*. Certain men have an insatiable lust for power and influence: in previous eras much of this drive was channelled into military endeavours. In the 21st century the empire building tends to be in the business arena, but the ruthless tactics and devices the experts recommend seem the same. Possibly Lord Acton was correct when he said: "Great men are almost always bad men."

August 2000

Old Raiders Face Music

In the 1980s a new breed appeared on Wall Street. The corporate raiders included men like T. Boone Pickens, Carl Icahn, Ron Perelman – and Saul Steinberg. These merciless capitalists terrorised corporate America by launching hostile bids for large, undervalued public companies – mostly using debt.

Steinberg, an early client and backer of Mike Milken and his junk bond empire, has been making headlines since the mid-1960s. He was born in middle-class comfort in Brooklyn in 1939, and attended Wharton Business School in Pennsylvania. There, while writing his thesis, he invented the concept of independent computer leasing, and in 1961 started Leasco with $25,000.

The company was successful from the start and went public in 1965. Its profits grew rapidly and the share price soared. In 1968 Leasco used its highly-rated shares to buy control of Reliance, an undervalued insurance company 10 times its size. In the five years to 1969 Leasco (to be renamed Reliance) shares rose 5,410 per cent, the greatest gain of any stock in the period, and Steinberg became the richest self-made American under 30 with net worth of $50m, according to *Forbes*.

In 1969, Steinberg and Reliance tried unsuccessfully to take control of Chemical Bank, then a $9bn corporation – one of the most shocking takeover attempts ever and one that demonstrated Steinberg's extraordinary boldness. Steinberg discovered, like Warren Buffett, that an insurance underwriter has a pool of capital which can be used for investment purposes, and these returns make or break the business. So effectively Reliance was both an insurer and an investor. Steinberg might chiefly be remembered in Britain for his bizarre run-in with Robert Maxwell. In a convoluted deal in 1969, Reliance bought 38 per cent of Pergamon Press, paying nearly £10m with a view to taking over the company. But he discovered the Pergamon books had been cooked and removed Maxwell from the board. The DTI undertook an inquiry and Maxwell was ousted and disgraced. But the deal was a financial disaster for Steinberg. Pergamon went downhill rapidly and he was forced to sell out to Maxwell in 1974, valuing his stake at just 5 per cent of its cost.

Reliance was taken private by Steinberg in 1982, in a deal financed by Drexel Burnham Lambert, after borrowing $500m in junk bonds. It refloated on the New York Stock Exchange in 1986 and its valued peaked at more than $2bn in 1998. Meanwhile, Steinberg became a part of the establishment. He owned a 34-room Park Avenue triplex apartment and more than 60 old master paintings. With his third wife, Gayfryd, he gave the grandest parties including one for his own 50th birthday on their estate in the Hamptons that the *New York Times* called "one of the 10 most memorable soirees of the 20th century".

But the last few years have been catastrophic for Steinberg and Reliance Group Holdings. He suffered a stroke in 1995 and is permanently disabled. Reliance shares have fallen from almost $20 in early 1998 to 25 cents today.

Earlier this week it announced a second-quarter loss of $504m and said it may go bankrupt. The company has made huge losses on reinsurance of workers' compensation claims and has liabilities which may exceed its assets – as well as $730m in debt. Steinberg is the largest loser since he and his family own 43 per cent of Reliance. One should not shed too many tears for the old raider. During his 31-year tenure at Reliance, it is estimated he took out $250m in salary and dividends, and enjoyed the corporate Boeing 727. Reliance still pays him a $635,000 pension.

But Steinberg is unlikely to enjoy a quiet retirement. The demise of Reliance will doubtless inspire rafts of shareholder and bondholder lawsuits that will follow him to the grave. It seems that despite his philanthropy, parties and illness, his aggression and greed will never be forgiven.

August 2000

Boards

The current havoc among Vodafone's management reveals the painful truth: business is more emotion than hard facts. Even in one of the biggest firms in the world.

Ultimately companies are built by egotists who want to change the world. No-one who takes the risks required to create a new enterprise does it because they are modest individuals. They do it because they want to be boss of something, and they want to upset the old order. This requires strength of character and an assertive personality. But one person alone can't construct a multinational: they need the support of thousands of staff and plenty of bright managers – probably some outside capital – and a board of fellow directors. And that's where the trouble can start

Now modern corporate boards are curious things. They are hardly democracies, but neither should they be dictatorships. Directors are divided between executives and non-executives – and then they have the Chief Executive and the Chairman. Archie Norman told me the Chairman should never be characterised as non-executive, but most are at best part-time. They do not run the company, but they do have three key roles: they hire (and perhaps fire) the CEO; they run the board; and they get actively involved in times of crisis, like a takeover bid or a financial disaster. Warren Buffett said the Chairman decides on capital allocation and motivates the business leaders. A good Chairman can be a real benefit to a business – a bad Chairman can cause chaos.

Greg Dyke recently wrote that the relationship between the CEO and Chairman is the most important one in any company. He may be right. I suspect his favourite Chairman was Sir Christopher Bland, who was Chair of both LWT and the BBC. No doubt he liked him because Bland showed him how to make £7 million out of the part take-private at LWT – and he made him Director General at the BBC. In fact Bland was a virtual full-timer at both TV organisations, but Dyke, educated in a state school, was always impressed by the super-posh establishment figure Sir Christopher. So their relationship worked well – cockney socialist and Tory grandee. Other duos at the top can find the going a little less smooth.

In warring boards, the row is usually between the Chair and the CEO. Such punch-ups invariably arise because of trading problems – in times of affluence, everyone tends to get on. The resentments and blame come out if things fall apart. Normally the Chair wins, but that isn't always the right outcome. The CEO typically has to fall on his sword because ultimately he takes responsibility for failure. Moreover, the Chair can usually count on the support of many of the non-executives, since he often hires them, and by so doing buys their allegiance. The resolution of the contest at GCap, the media business, was a recent example. The board and shareholders backed Ralph Barnard last year over David Mansfield, following the merger of GWR and Capital Radio.

Inevitably most boards of major undertakings are dominated by alpha males, so the testosterone often gets in the way of sensible decision making. I suspect female-dominated boards suffer less from harmful office politics. The sort of skulduggery that goes on in FTSE companies makes the political machinations of Imperial Rome look tame, save for the fact that the departing losers get hefty pay-offs these days – rather than being executed. It's as if certain boards are guided by intuitive, right-brain thinking, rather than analytical, left-brain thinking. Whether this makes them more successful is highly debatable. It certainly makes boardrooms more volatile and unpredictable places. Perhaps corporate high flyers need high drama and intrigue to make their lives more exciting. I guess the daily grind of meetings and phone calls is enlivened by a decent power struggle or conspiracy now and then.

The best boards work as a team, where the non-executives champion and support the executives. They should supervise and scrutinize, but must not undermine, and never criticize the management outside the confines of the executive suite. As one generation passes the baton to the next, these rules are often broken while the old guard are cleared out.

March 2006

Buzzwords

To liven up long workdays, practitioners in business and finance have always coined their own slang. Some of it is irritating and trite, but some is invigorating and shows English is a living, evolving language. I've gathered here a selection of some of the more imaginative and bizarre words and phrases capitalists use:

Jennifer syndrome: the tendency for rich men to show off to their second, trophy wives by doing silly things they think are manly e.g. buying motorbikes, corporate jets, getting into rows in restaurants etc.

Meeting Moth: executive who flits from meeting to meeting but actually does nothing useful.

Killer Bees: investment bankers who help defend target companies from hostile takeovers, using all sorts of clever tactics like making inappropriate acquisitions as a poison pill.

Melpew: the language of the fast food industry – a contraction of the phrase 'May I help you?'

Blamestorming: similar to brainstorming but designed specifically to pick a scapegoat for any problems.

Alligator Property: a piece of real estate which makes a net loss on all the outgoings – mortgage repayments, repairs, and rates – and so gradually eats up any equity. Likely to be common in buy-to-let situations if residential values fall.

Empty Suit: a yes man who fancies himself as a leader. He has little talent and no opinions, but crawls to superiors well and plays office politics with great skill.

Director of First Impressions: the receptionist.

Ankle Biter: small public company that is coming from behind, employing the Avis strategy 'We Try Harder' against its larger rivals.

Percussive Maintenance: the tactic of hitting a machine to make it work e.g. a car or computer.

Ubiquity factor: propensity for certain people to succeed simply by always showing up. They will always attend that crucial meeting you had to miss.

Elephant Man Strategy: a scheme simply too scary to back, even if it sounds incredibly exciting. The Channel Tunnel is an example.

All Flash, No Cash: the financial equivalent of 'All Talk, No Trousers'.

Beverage leadership: the person who gets the coffee at the office.

Greenwash: a company that touts its environmental credentials to deflect attention from other, less attractive aspects of its operations.

Accounting Noise: the current mess of confusing financial statements, created by a combination of excessive rules, and occasionally management manipulation. It is necessary to cut through the noise to really understand the underlying performance of a business.

Moonshine Shop: the research and development department.

Mad Hatter: an irresponsible Chief Executive, styled after the tea party character in 'Alice's Adventures in Wonderland' who asked riddles with no answers.

Administrivia: the bureaucratic sludge that buries anyone who works in most large organisations, especially those in the public sector.

Pitt Principle: the deliberate hiring of an incompetent in a regulatory role. Practised by various investment firms with their compliance officers.

Kitchen Sinking: policy adopted by incoming Chief Executives to troubled companies, whereby they deliberately overstate losses in order to make any recovery they engineer look all the better.

Mexican Standoff: legal device to ensure joint venture partners cannot rip each other off – both parties are required to make a best offer for the other's share – the higher bidder wins.

Bloatation: the process of hiring lots of useless senior staff immediately prior to going bust.

Safety Droids: tedious Health & Safety managers who go around highlighting the tiniest risks.

Bobbleheading: mass nodding by staff in a meeting at a remark by the boss that no-one understands.

November 2006

Selling

When I was nineteen I spent a summer working the phones in a 'pen room' in Beverly Hills, California. I worked as a commission-only salesman, cold-calling firms listed in the Yellow Pages all across America, trying to persuade them to buy personalised ball-point pens. We read from a script, and if my patter was faltering, the boss grabbed the receiver and closed the sale. He was one of the most compelling salesmen I've ever met. He had none of the embarrassment over selling so prevalent this side of the Atlantic. The experience taught me first hand that selling is at the root of US capitalism.

In the late 19th and early 20th centuries, a series of huge manufacturing concerns were founded in America that pioneered modern sales management. Mass marketing followed the rise of mass production. Firms like Eastman Kodak, Coca-Cola, Wrigley's and Heinz used armies of salesmen to push their wares across the country. The real trailblazer was John H. Patterson, a former coal dealer from Ohio. He bought control of National Cash Registers, and invented the technique of 'scientific salesmanship' to find buyers for his machines. He was not a nice man, but a hugely effective promoter of his products. He introduced prepared sales routines and systematic bonus schemes. NCR fostered a whole generation of talented managers who went on to lead corporations like General Motors and IBM, where they applied its sales methods religiously. The peddlers and canvassers of previous generations became sales executives, with territories, quotas, prospecting, referrals and all the other paraphernalia of the salesman. The profession of selling was born.

Within a couple of decades, advertising similarly came of age. Again, Americans embraced the discipline with a vigour sadly lacking in Britain. We have always been somewhat schizophrenic about such activities. On the one hand, we launched the industrial revolution in the 18th century, and ushered in the capitalist era. Yet as a nation we are remarkably squeamish about the whole art of selling things for a profit. It is as if an aristocratic disdain for 'trade' still lingers in our culture. Only an American like Dale Carnegie could have written *How to Win Friends and Influence People*, perhaps the best selling sales manual ever. In Britain, publishers in 1937 would have sneered and turned down his manuscript.

With the rise of salesmanship in the 1900s came advances in commerce: brands, real competition, improvements in packaging and self-service retailing. New branches of academia sprang up around the phenomenon of selling: market research, consumer behaviour and industrial psychology. Meanwhile other spin-offs were created: national magazines, and in due course, national radio and television networks, to run advertising to sell the output of America's factories. And distribution methods evolved: in the fifteen years from 1914 to 1929, the numbers of trucks delivering goods to the nation's stores increased forty-fold. The age of the consumer had arrived.

There are probably as many travelling salesmen (or women) as ever in the 21st century, but nowadays in fields like pharmaceuticals and computer software. Their mission remains the same: to convince people to try new products, and keep the whole system moving. In Arthur Miller's play *Death of a Salesman*, Willy Loman is described by a friend: "He's a man way out there in the blue, riding on a smile and a shoeshine...A salesman is got to dream boy. It comes with the territory." I've never met a successful entrepreneur who isn't a natural at sales – and a dreamer. Without that sort of belief, no-one would be mad enough to start a business.

At its heart selling remains the essence of capitalism: the customer gets to pick from a variety of products – and has to be convinced of the merits of a particular item before purchasing it. Thus the buyer has freedom of choice. Whereas in the public sector – health, education, the police and so forth – the state is for most of us a monopoly supplier, that can only operate by expropriation of funds through compulsory taxation. The former is run by owners who must make a return by generating repeat business from willing customers, against competition. The latter is led by politicians whose prime objective is getting re-elected once every five years and serving their party. Having to sell in the marketplace makes organisations fit and lean. Being a monopoly provider does the opposite. I salute the salesmen, who keep the show on the road.

November 2006

3

Winners

World-Beating, Single-Product Companies

If you want to denigrate a business, you dismiss it with the line: "Ah, but it's a single product company." Such a put-down consigns the enterprise to a limited future and a risky reliance on just one source of income. Surely it is better to enjoy a diversity of revenues and a balanced portfolio of goods for sale? Not always, perhaps. There are a few small, perfectly-formed multinationals that only produce one thing – but do it so well that they enjoy success in many markets over the world.

Perhaps my favourite example is Illycaffe SpA, the wonderful espresso coffee maker from northern Italy. They have been headquartered in Trieste, on the Adriatic, for over 70 years. This evocative port city is a centre for the coffee trade and it was here in 1933 that a Hungarian émigré called Francesco Illy started a coffee trading company. Since then Illy has grown to become perhaps the elite of all coffee brands. Today it supplies many of the finest restaurants, cafés and hotels all over the globe. They sell just one superlative blend, made up of 100% Arabica beans, the more subtle and aromatic coffee bean. Others, like Starbucks, flog many different blends and products: at Illy, they concentrate on making sure their single espresso blend is always the finest, while converting more customers to its merits.

The business is still a private company and remains family owned and run, despite achieving annual revenues in excess of $175 million. That makes it a relatively small competitor beside industry giants like Lavazza or Nestlé, but most experts agree that no-one matches Illy's coffee for consistency and quality. The current Chief Executive is urbane Dr. Andréa Illy, a chemist by background, who continues the family tradition of innovation and passionate focus on the product. He has even authored a textbook on the science of coffee. Illy helped pioneer the technology of the automatic espresso machine which has now conquered the world, and invented a new pressurized method to store coffee and keep it fresh. They also market an inspiring range of coffee cups designed by famous artists. Every day over five million people drink their delicious, single roast in over 70 countries.

Another international niche company is The Economist Group, a British winner. Their principal eponymous title has been published continuously in London since 1843, founded to participate in "a severe contest between intelligence, which presses forward, and an unworthy, timid ignorance obstructing our progress." The flagship magazine remains their single key product, and has recently climbed to an all-time high circulation of over one million copies a week in more than 50 countries. Despite a prolonged media recession in recent times, during the last five years the firm has grown operating margins from under 8% in 2001 to almost 14% in 2005, when profits reached a record £27 million on revenues of £197 million. During that period net assets trebled and earnings per share doubled.

The Economist's impressive performance stands in stark contrast to the pedestrian results of *The Financial Times*, the other famous UK publication covering business and commerce. The former is an independent company but 50% owned by Pearson; the *FT* is a 100% subsidiary of the publishing conglomerate. Perhaps *The Economist* benefits from its strong stance on free markets, globalisation and economic liberalism. The *FT*, on the other hand, frequently seems to forget that its readers buy it in order to make money – not to receive condescending lectures about the wonders of the EU or the genius of New Labour.

While The Economist Group also owns The Economist Intelligence Unit and *CFO* magazine, it is still essentially a one-product business – but a brilliantly successful one at that. It sells 80% of its copies overseas and derives roughly half of its income from subscriptions and half from advertising sales. Its articles almost never carry a byline and its quirky, authoritative tone means it is taken seriously by readers and advertisers in boardrooms, universities and governments.

Both Illy and The Economist Group offer premium products and charge accordingly. The businesses are managed for the long-term and enjoy their status as private companies, not forced to kow-tow to stock markets or private equity masters. Both have very high reputations within their sectors, nurtured across many territories over many years. They each compete against much larger rivals, but with a dedication towards excellence both have achieved world-class status despite modest capital bases. Their progress should serve as a lesson in how to build single-product, global brands.

August 2005

It is refreshing to see the Financial Times, under a new editor, recall its core readership and so enjoy renewed success in circulation terms.

Champagne

Champagne, more than perfume, posh luggage or haute couture, epitomises the French luxury goods industry. It can only be produced in a certain region of France, near Reims and Epernay; it is dramatically more expensive than rival sparkling wines, like cava from Spain; and it has an image of glamour and celebration which is hard to match.

It was reputedly invented by a Benedictine monk called Dom Perignon in the late 17th Century. He was the procureur of the Abbey of Hautvillers and pioneered the crucial second fermentation, which produces the carbon dioxide that gives champagne its bubbles. The business retains a highly traditional structure in many respects, and is intricately organised. It is a long-term craft that requires patient capital, and is composed of 19,000 mostly small growers who produce grapes, and 4,000 producers. There is little of the mechanisation which has transformed wine production in many countries in recent years. Productivity remains pretty low, and despite a trebling of hectares devoted to champagne grapes over the decades, most houses still operate at close to capacity.

Inevitably there has been consolidation. While there are as many as 10,000 champagne brands, the export trade is dominated by the 24 grand marques. Among them, the major players are LVMH, Marne et Champagne, Vranken Monopole and Laurent Perrier. Together these four giants represent almost a third of the entire market. A few like Bollinger remain family owned. Meanwhile smaller groups band together in co-operatives. Yet the multinationals only control 13% of the vineyards, and still rely upon the smallholders to provide grapes, the essence of any champagne.

Overall, French consumption still dominates the total market – they buy almost two-thirds of the roughly 300 million bottles sold every year. The two big export markets are Britain and the US. We drink almost twice as much as the Americans, a remarkable statistic considering they have five times our population. Moreover, Britain remains the fastest growing champagne market in the world – it seems we enjoy conspicuous consumption more than most! The value of the champagne market in Britain has grown by 50% since 1998 to around £1.2 billion, while the value of the total industry is at least £5 billion.

Unlike the mainstream French wine trade, the champagne industry has substantially avoided the ferocious export competition from New World suppliers. Many countries produce sparkling wines: Germany has sekt, Spain cava, Italy prosecco, South Africa Cap Classique and so forth. But Champagne dominates. It has two-thirds by value of the world market for sparkling wines, although only a quarter by volume. The Italians have 40% of the volume but just 15% by value, while Spain has 18% by volume and 10% by value. The French capture almost the entire premium end.

The fact is champagne has been brilliantly marketed over the decades, and it has succeeded in retaining a cache while French still wine has lost reputation and export market share. The Comite Interprofessional du Vin de Champagne, the organisation of growers and producers, has promoted and protected the reputation and integrity of champagne. The grand marques invest in advertising, public relations, design and packaging, and it pays. The quality of many sparkling wines produced elsewhere matches that of champagne but the French have managed to sell the intangible delights of their effervescent alcohol far more effectively than their rivals from Spain, Italy, California, Australia and South Africa. The high selling prices and growth in demand for sparking wines mean many vineyards and bottlers would love to steal some of the champagne's market share – but it has proved a resilient category.

While champagne remains market leader, its position is not unassailable. It is an expensive product – partly because it is produced in a cumbersome way, partly because the public expects it to be pricey. Most houses and growers do not make substantial profits or margins – costs in the Champagne province are too high for that. Moreover, the growth in sales of cheaper, own-label champagnes may start to undermine its market. There is unquestionably a considerable opportunity for higher quality rivals to steal champagne's market share. The rapid growth in sales of cava in Britain in the last few years shows how drinkers' tastes can change. Cava is made using modern industrial methods and yet quality has been maintained. The producers of champagne cannot afford to be complacent. They have to tread a fine line between selectivity and volume; keeping the kudos of the 'methode champagnoise' while ensuring production is efficient; and maintaining the reputations and quality of the grand marques which act as flagships for the drink.

Champagne is an ingenious product and a true French success story. It will be fascinating to see if the industry manages to hold on to its privileged position in the years to come.

March 2006

Ineos

Seismic shifts are taking place in the way capitalism is carried out in the West. For a case study, look no further than the British chemical industry. It demonstrates starkly how heritage, quoted equity and prudence count for little these days – and how ambition, debt and an appetite for risk are everything.

Imperial Chemical Industries was formed in October 1926 from a four-way merger of Nobel Industries, Brunner Mond, United Alkali and British Dyestuffs. It remained a bellwether of British business and a core component of the London Stock Exchange from its creation for over 60 years. But a few years ago incompetent management, a huge restructuring programme and a cyclical downturn brought the company to its knees. It demerged the pharmaceutical division Zeneca, which rapidly overtook its parent in value and profits. Poorly-timed acquisitions, funded with debt, saw the firm forced into firesale disposals and a collapsing share price. Despite huge resources and commanding market positions, somehow ICI found itself needing an £800 million rescue rights issue in early 2002, when its market value had fallen to a desperate £1.5 billion, against borrowings of £2.9 billion.

ICI embarked on a flawed strategy to exit bulk industrial chemicals and grow speciality chemicals after buying various Unilever assets for a rich price. Now it is a shadow of its former self, with a share price no higher than five years ago, earnings stagnant and lower sales than in 2001. And this is after a share price recovery of 60% in the last 12 months! Its website touts 'Creating value' as a core mission – but ICI has suffered terrible leadership and a profound lack of strategic vision in recent times. The company might boast a board with 11 grandees, including a Lord and a Baroness, and a splendid head office in London's West End, but they have generated poor returns for investors for many years.

Yet during this sad decline, down in modest premises in

Hampshire, an industrial chemicals giant was being simultaneously assembled. From a standing start in 1998 – just about the time ICI started to implode – an engineer called Jim Ratcliffe has built the world's third largest chemical business, Ineos. This company is extremely private, with Chairman Ratcliffe still owning 57% of it, while the rest is in the hands of the staff. It has been constructed using bank debt and high yield bonds, and by buying orphan assets in speciality and intermediate chemicals from old line public companies. Ratcliffe worked at Esso and Courtaulds before moving to the private equity industry with Advent, where he learnt the power of leverage. He enjoyed major success in the 1990s with Inspec, a public company whose value grew 15 fold before it was sold off. He took the proceeds from this and then embarked on an amazing expansion spree.

In the last eight years Ineos has carried out an array of purchases of companies making products like acrylics, oxides, silicas, phenols, vinyls, glycols and chlorines. It bought these businesses from ICI, Dow Chemical, BASF, BP and Degussa. Last December it pulled off a blockbuster deal: the $9 billion purchase of BP's petrochemical assets, an operation called Innovene. This took the annual revenues of Ineos to $33 billion, generated by 68 facilities in 14 countries, manned by almost 16,000 employees.

Determining the company's debt and profitability is difficult, but it probably carries at least $10 billion of borrowings of one sort or another, and could make EBITDA of perhaps $2 billion. It has been backed by blue chip names like Barclays Capital, Merrill Lynch and Morgan Stanley. Ineos appears to have bought cheaply and timed its acquisitions well, while cutting costs and using the improved profitability and cash generation to borrow more. If the Innovene deal really works, the equity of Ineos could quite easily be worth more than ICI in a couple of years: already its enterprise value and revenues are greater.

Thus several billion pounds of value will have been created by Ineos in less than a decade. Yet despite such advantages as covenant, capital, billions of assets and unimpeachable respectability, cumbersome public companies like ICI are being left in the slow lane. Once more it has been firmly demonstrated that enterprise and boldness are far more important to success than blue chip membership of the industrial establishment. The quoted company model is not quite dead, but it still defies belief that upstart firms like Ineos can seize such opportunities, while their aristocratic peers like ICI drift and degear just at the wrong point in the cycle.

May 2006

Digital Radio

Occasionally one comes across a new technology that is really exciting. I've recently made just such a discovery: digital radio. I was lucky enough to be given a Digital Audio Broadcasting (DAB) radio as a Christmas present, and I predict this will be the hit new phenomenon of 2003. Moreover, it is an innovation where Britain is a world leader.

The advantages of DAB radio compared to conventional AM/FM broadcasts are immediately apparent. The sound quality is considerably better: this is especially so for spoken word and classical music transmissions. For example, BBC Radio 3, which always has interference on FM, sounds superb on DAB. Another real plus of DAB is the simplicity: you just twist the dial until you see on the LCD screen the name of your chosen station, and then stop. You never need re-tune. A further benefit is the expanded choice of stations. Already there are 300 stations – many unique to DAB, appealing to specialist audiences – both local and national. Because of the extra room for signals using DAB technology, there should ultimately be hundreds more stations without overcrowding the airwaves.

A unique feature of DAB radio is the opportunity for broadcasters to transmit text onto your radio's display screen, so telling you for example the name of the song currently being played, results of sports matches and so forth. Features such as the ability to retrieve information and record and store broadcasts are likely to be added as time goes on.

Every single person to whom I've demonstrated DAB has been impressed and wants to get a DAB radio. The fantastic thing about radio is that once you've bought the receiver, everything else is free: this isn't like new digital television channels, where you pay a subscription, or mobile phones where you pay for calls, or even terrestrial television where you pay for a licence. Currently most of the receivers are expensive, but the Evoke-1 receiver only costs £99, and is an elegant, retro design and portable. Unfortunately you cannot currently easily buy this radio: every single retailer in the country seems to have sold out.

The maker of this set goes under the brand Pure Digital – and is part of an obscure public company called Imagination Technologies Group PLC. It used to be called VideoLogic Systems and enjoyed a share price of over 600p and a P/E multiple of 200 a couple of years ago. These days its shares fetch about 18p and sit close to an all-time low, with a market value of around £30 million. Although it makes losses, it has £5 million in net cash and an array of different intellectual property in areas such as 3D graphics, and DAB. It licenses much of this to semiconductor multinationals such as Intel and Hitachi. Its silicon and software technologies go into consumer electronics like game consoles, mobiles and PDAs. An investment in its shares would be highly speculative, but it is a leader in DAB technology and should do well out of it thanks to the UK's world lead in rolling out digital radio. Moreover, I notice several Directors have bought shares recently.

It sells its technology to Alba plc, a successful maker of consumer equipment like TVs, hi-fi and radios. Alba itself sells various DAB devices under the Goodman brand. Its shares are around 380p and its profits are expected to recover sharply in the current financial year to March 31st to an all-time record. While DAB products will only be a small proportion of its projected profits of £25 million, it has gained an important edge ahead of rivals. Its shares are on a fair multiple of 10.

Another way of playing digital radio is the shares of GWR. They have more commercial radio station licences and a bigger radio audience than any other broadcaster. They own Classic FM and channels Core and Planet Rock, and a 63% stake in Digital One, the UK's only national digital commercial network, held under a 12 year licence. At 132p the shares are on a lofty 25 prospective earnings, but they do have 16 digital radio licences and will benefit enormously if digital listening really takes off. Inevitably, they are a geared play on an advertising recovery, and they also have a not insubstantial £120 million of debt.

In a few years we shall all do our radio listening using digital sets. Groups like the BBC have invested millions in DAB stations, including new ones such as BBC 7. Digital will become mainstream as users get DAB devices in cars and realise the advantages, and when receivers fall in price. Current audiences are pathetic, but this will change quickly as early adopters talk about it. Like so much technology, the future of radio is digital.

February 2003

The growth of DAB radio has been relentless. Over one million PURE radio sets have been sold – and two million DAB radios in total in 2006 alone. Over 15% of homes now have digital radio, and over 50% are expected to have adopted it by 2010. Sets now start at £29 and many car makers now provide a DAB listening option. Meanwhile there are more DAB radio stations than ever and listening figures keep on climbing. And Imagination Technologies shares have risen from 18p to 130p currently. While commercial FM radio stations have struggled in the last couple of years thanks to the threat from online advertising, investment in digital radio continues apace, and the UK remains the world leader.

Air Conditioning

I learned the importance air conditioning in a humid climate when I helped establish a factory in Brunswick, Georgia about ten years ago. Our firm took over a brand new plant with top of the range cooling systems, but no workers. Directly opposite stood a facility operated by a rival with 400 staff and no air conditioning. We opened for business in June and by July half of our competitor's staff had walked across the road to come and work for us at the same wage because conditions in our building were so much more pleasant.

Air conditioning was truly one of the most important inventions of the twentieth century. From the beginning it was an American concept: the pioneer was a remarkable physician called John Gorrie, from tropical Apalachicola, Florida. He worked as postmaster, town councillor, treasurer, bank director and mayor before focusing his energies on the idea of controlling urban climates for the improvement of health. In 1842 he wrote a paper entitled 'Refrigeration and Ventilation in Cities', and spent the rest of his life until he died in 1855 inventing various devices, such as the Gorrie Ice Machine, to cool society.

Further advances were achieved by engineer Alfred R. Woolff, who installed comfort cooling in the dissecting room of the Cornell Medical College Building in New York in 1899. His fifty-ton refrigeration machine was designed to keep the corpses chilled. The system proved so refreshing that graduation exercises were subsequently held in the slightly macabre surroundings of the air-cooled dissecting room.

But it took almost fifty years from Gorrie's death for the real breakthrough to come about. In 1902, Dr Willis Carrier, an engineer just out of Cornell University earning just $10 a week, invented a mechanism he called process cooling, for use in a printing plant in Brooklyn. Reputedly he had his brainwave while waiting for his train on a cold, foggy night. He patented his 'Apparatus for Testing Air' four years later and kick-started an entire industry. Carrier employed a centrifugal system that used the evaporation of a refrigerant liquid to cool and dehumidify the environment. Willis Haviland Carrier was a classic practical American man of action. He said: "I fish only for edible fish, and hunt only for edible game, even in the laboratory." Remarkably, the business he founded remains the world leader today, an $11 billion division of United Technologies Corporation. Not bad for a business incorporated in 1915 with capital of just $35,000.

Initially mechanical cooling was called 'manufactured weather' and it took off slowly. It only achieved large scale popularity in the 1920s, when theatres saw the economic value of air conditioning: by 1938, around 15,000 of America's cinemas had installed it. Freon, the ubiquitous refrigerant, replaced the early, somewhat dangerous volatile fluids in 1930. Meanwhile, more and more offices, factories and department stores were enjoying the advantages of climate control.

Carrier died in 1950. Over the next few years the air conditioning age started in earnest. It became the second fastest growing US industry after television: in 1952 there were 20 companies in the business; two years later there were 92. Architects and builders took to specify air conditioning in new structures, and in 1956 Victor Gruen opened the first shopping mall in Edina, Minneapolis, inspired by the idea of a controlled environment: an enclosed, air conditioned retail space. By 1960, over 12% of American homes were air conditioned: twenty years later the figure was 55%.

Air conditioning spread from commercial buildings to houses and cars, trains and planes, allowing people to live, work and travel comfortably in hot and cold weather. It is arguable that by pioneering and embracing air conditioning, America accelerated its economic development. It permitted more efficient, productive working and living conditions for tens of millions of citizens. The relative economic performance of the Deep South against America's North-East accelerated noticeably following WWII and the widespread introduction of air conditioning. Indeed, many

Southerners think that next to the Civil War the most important event in history was the invention of air conditioning. Plenty believe India's growth would exceed China's if it could only get enough air conditioning working.

Henry Miller wrote a critique of American culture in 1945 called *The Air Conditioned Nightmare*. More recently, environmentalists have complained about the damage refrigerants might cause the ozone layer. But you only have to experience a really muggy day in the city to understand that air conditioning is actually the essence of the American Dream: a brilliant innovation which has made everyday life incomparably better for untold millions.

August 2005

Trademark Companies

Registered trademarks are normally associated with a single product or brand, but sometimes they represent an entire company. I've noticed three highly successful such firms, each dominant in its niche, founded on genuine technology by true inventors.

The first is Muzak. It is the world leader in piped music, supplied to shops, restaurants, hotels and offices – and of course elevators. It was started by retired Major General George O. Squier in 1922, who patented the technique of transmitting music over power lines. He named his invention after a combination of 'music' and 'Kodak' – his favourite business. A huge public utility corporation called North American Company acquired exclusive rights and started marketing its service to hotels in New York, supplying easy listening music over phone lines. It hit the big time when its calm vibes soothed passengers travelling in lifts up tall skyscrapers.

Over the decades the business had many owners: Warner Brothers, William Benton (founder of Benton & Bowles), Wrather Corporation, TelePrompter, Westinghouse, and Marshall Field V. It grew and evolved, supplying more commercial premises with an ever greater choice of music, and was even piped into the White House on the instructions of Eisenhower. It remains a private company, now controlled by ABRY Partners out of Boston. These days it mostly distributes its tunes via satellite, and has over half the market for background music. Every day over 100 million people listen to its output; it has 350,000 clients and 3,000 employees. It prefers to call itself an 'audio imaging company' and a 'global icon', and believes its products and services can enhance sales, by providing customised music and using 'audio architecture and audio branding'. It enjoys revenues of almost $250 million and EBITDA in 2004 of $65 million, although it also carries total debt of over $430 million – mostly junk bonds. It also has a very groovy website at www.muzak.com

A second specialist business with an instantly recognisable name – and which remains an independent company – is Velcro. The original product was invented in 1948 by a Swiss engineer called George de Mestral. He noticed while walking his dog how burrs would entangle in the animal's fur, and under a microscope saw how the hooks fastened on to the dog's coat – and copied the principle with man-made fibres. These days the business is called Velcro Industries NV, and it is a leader in hook and loop fasteners of all different descriptions. They have been constant technical innovators and have operations across the globe.

Velcro Industries NV has a quotation on NASDAQ, but only just, since a mere 4% of the equity is held by outsiders. The balance appears to be owned by the family of Sir Humphrey Cripps. He was a successful British entrepreneur who died in 2000. The company itself is registered in the tax haven of Curacao, Netherland Antilles. The business is valued at $406 million, and generates revenues of around $280 million and operating profits of $46 million. Operating profit margins of 16% in the textile industry are enviable, and can only be achieved thanks to the patent and brand name assets possessed by Velcro. The company supplies its products to the automotive, industrial and consumer markets, and all use its ingenious fastening technology.

The third company which caught my eye is Dolby Laboratories, the pioneer in noise reduction for recorded sound. Dolby got rid of the 'hiss' on magnetic tape. The business was founded by American engineer Ray Dolby in London on 17th May 1965, after a PhD at Cambridge University. Previously he was part of the team that invented the video tape recorder at Ampex in 1956. Dolby Labs is another business built upon ground-breaking intellectual property. It diversified away from servicing the music recording industry and expanded in the movie business. Now, virtually every film soundtrack is encoded using Dolby technology, as are most DVDs. While a proportion of their revenues are made directly from sales of products and services, most comes from licensing income.

The business moved from Clapham to San Francisco in 1976 and finally went public on the NYSE in February this year, with Mr Dolby still the principal owner. It's currently capitalised at almost $1.5 billion, with historic revenues of $289 million and pre-tax profits of over $100 million. While the multiple isn't cheap, investors obviously like the fact that almost three quarters of sales come from royalty income. Dolby is yet another global winner based on superior intellectual property.

September 2005

Book Publishing

They say there are three ways of achieving immortality: rear a child, plant a tree, or write a book. Quite a few of us seem to be having a go at the third category – over a million titles a year are published around the world, according to the appropriately named book *So Many Books* by Mexican Gabriel Zaid. This never-ending volcano of reading matter means book publishing is a wonderful service to the literary pubic, but a poorly paid profession and generally a terrible business.

Books are curious things. We publish over 125,000 new titles a year in Britain – more than any other nation of a comparable size – yet books are much less perishable than most other forms of media, be they newspapers, magazines, radio, television, even films. Book publishing can work as a craft trade, such that specialist titles appealing to only 2,000 readers can be economically viable. By contrast, substantial capital investment means computer games, TV shows, theatre productions, music albums and so forth have to appeal to much bigger audiences to get financed.

Book publishing really is somewhere between art and commerce – in some aspects it is a barely rational industry. While the big four publishers have half the British market, the rest is fragmented into hundreds of small players. Few who have much to do with books make a good living out of it – and this despite the fact that books in English represent 27% of the world's share of titles! Most authors receive pitiful advances which are rarely earned out. Salaries among staff in publishing houses are notoriously low. And owners of imprints must mostly do it for love, since it is an endemically unprofitable industry.

I owned a book publisher for a period and found it a painful experience. I learned that the cashflow characteristics are most unattractive. You pay authors up front for manuscripts that might not arrive for years; you then ship finished volumes to booksellers who only accept them on a sale or return basis, and demand at least 55% trade discount, and pay 120 days later. Most titles on a publisher's list lose money and sell at most a few thousand copies – editors are perpetually searching feverishly for the elusive bestseller to pay for all the flops. It is a Winner Takes All business. Occasionally there are windfalls from foreign or film rights, and backlists provide a degree of long-term income. But even giant trade publishers only make 5% operating margins, despite spin-off benefits and global scale at multi-media conglomerates like Bertelsmann, News Corporation, Pearson and Time Warner.

Of course that is part of the reason book publishing is so tough: it is ferociously competitive because so many participants do it for uneconomic reasons. They understand that books are central to civilization, representing a more profound form of culture than all the other mass media put together. We do at least buy many more books than we used to – but actually read a lower proportion of them. Sadly for the book trade, persistent price deflation means the production efficiencies of technology advances in pre-press, printing, binding and logistics have all been given away to the reading public. Moreover in Britain, enormous concentration of power among chain retailers like WHSmiths, Waterstones, Borders and Ottakar's means there are now only a handful of powerful customers who demand ever better terms from suppliers. Even the emergence of online sellers like Amazon hasn't really helped: they insist on a wholesaler's discount and undermine the sale of full-price copies. And 20% of Amazon's sales are now used books, a huge stimulus to the second hand trade which doesn't help new book publishers.

The internet poses perhaps the greatest threat to the book, and yet the roughly 5% annual growth in the value of the British book market in recent years suggests it is faring better than the music business has. Books have advantages: they are portable, collectable, cheap and can be skimmed. Even sales of reference books have risen in the last few years, despite the cornucopia of free information available on the web. Unlike markets such as retailing, for the book trade progress has increased diversity and that is probably a strength. New titles, formats and imprints help keep the business vigorous – as does originality. Ultimately British book publishing will only be successful if it is original and creative: be it Lord of the Rings or Harry Potter, books can generate ideas and stories that fuel all other forms of entertainment. Derivative content will never grow the industry – fresh talent and concepts alone will keep it alive.

December 2004

4

Problems

What Can Go Wrong

Certain naïve people – some politicians and journalists, for example – see the capitalist's lot as a cushy number. They believe business owners have it easy, and are under-worked and over-rewarded in our materialistic society. They should try employing people and actually building an enterprise, and taste the grief first hand. On some days as an entrepreneur, it can feel as if the entire universe is conspiring to bring about your ruin. I'm quite sure research would show that the self-employed suffer more stress and anxiety-related diseases than others – even if they can't afford to take the time off sick. I noted down just 50 of the myriad difficulties that have beset me or those in business I have known – usually several problems at a time. Just to depress you, I list them here:

- Key executive becomes ill and is unable to work
- Major fraud discovered in accounting department
- Increase in tax
- Suppliers raise prices
- Competitors cut prices
- Rents go up
- Litigation from a customer
- Unfair dismissal claim from staff member
- IT systems crash
- Interest rates rise, increasing cost of debt
- Bad PR from product problems
- Products are replicated by rivals
- Important staff are poached by rival
- Exchange rates move wrong way
- Unseasonal weather ruins harvest/cuts demand
- New technology makes your products redundant
- Demand for big hike in pay by staff

- Cannot recruit qualified staff
- Customer goes bust and fails to pay
- Supplier refuses credit so squeezing working capital
- New regulations increase cost of doing business
- Disputes between owners
- Major fire/flood/theft in key premises
- Critical supplier goes bust
- New product launch fails to take off
- Products affected by health scare
- New plant/store/office goes over budget
- Terrorism outrage
- Low cost overseas competitors
- Old stock proves useless and has to be written off
- Theft and shrinkage of stock
- Machines break down and need replacing
- Deficit emerges in pension fund
- Lawsuit from unhappy shareholder
- Staff go on strike
- Overstated debtors
- Understated creditors
- Dilapidations claim from landlord
- Prosecution over pollution problem
- Hostile takeover bid
- Bank pulls plug on borrowing facilities
- Warranty claims from defective products
- Blacklisted by credit insurer
- Rival goes bust and receiver slashes prices in liquidation
- Assigned lease reverts when sub-tenant goes under
- Underinsured, so major claim fails
- Divorce forces disposal at wrong moment

- Senior staff have affair and then row
- Competitor infringes patent and plagiarises product
- Overseas customers/suppliers affected by political unrest

Perhaps Thoreau was referring not to employees but entrepreneurs when he said: "The mass of men lead lives of quiet desperation." They lay up "treasures which moth and rust will corrupt and thieves break through and steal. It is a fool's life, as they will find out when they get to the end of it, if not before." No-one is forced to start an enterprise of course – but if no-one ever did, how would we pay for the schools and hospitals? Would everyone work for the government? Running a company is a form of madness – and an addictive one. Once someone has tasted the freedom and satisfaction of making their own way in the world, and the fulfilment to be gained from building a business, they rarely surrender and re-enter the workforce. Despite all the hurdles and pitfalls, the desire to control one's own destiny is a powerful urge among certain wilful individuals – and society and the rest of us are the real beneficiaries.

January 2005

Things Fall Apart

Humans are rational, and therefore we try to organise things logically. This includes the business of prediction. We believe we can plan in a systematic way for the future. But the harsh truth of reality keeps intruding on our projections. As economist Paul Ormerod says in his new book, *Why Most Things Fail,* "intent is not the same as outcome."

In fact, it is the failures which permit the ultimate successes. This dictum applies in the evolution of firms just as it does to organisms. Economics in this sense is not very different from biology. Extinction at the level of the individual can benefit the system as a whole. So it should be no surprise that most ventures go wrong and that a tiny number of companies last very long.

In the restaurant trade, a handful of places last more than a few years. Tastes change, staff move on, owners get bored, new rivals open. It constantly astonishes me that our restaurants Le Caprice and J. Sheekey have been trading since 1947 and 1896 respectively. Of the world's 100 largest industrial companies in 1912, only nineteen were still at the top by 1995. Disappearance and decline of specific businesses is to be expected – even as the system shows huge growth.

Many believe the secret to a higher standard of living is productivity growth. This can only be achieved by constantly discovering new and more efficient ways of doing things. In turn this happens through trial and error: a constant struggle of life and death in the marketplace, competition relentlessly weeding out the weak or the stagnant who fail to evolve.

One of the causes of decline I call 'Pioneer's Curse'. This is the fate that befalls many early movers when they are leapfrogged by copycats – using their predecessor's hard-won experience. The pioneers suffer from the legacy investment, and perhaps inertia which prevents them from updating to cope with dynamic conditions. Thus, the London Underground in 1863 was the first subterranean urban railway in the world – a true innovation. They chose to bore single track tunnels using existing technology, rather than excavate trenches – which permitted double-track tunnels – as they have in the New York Subway and Paris Metro. Hence the Tube is too narrow to install air conditioning and other modernising features which would make journeys much more bearable.

Another example is the story of the De Havilland Comet. This was the world's first jet airliner – highly innovative, and designed and built in Britain. Tragically, the planes developed metal fatigue, and after three crashes they were withdrawn from service in 1954. By the time Comets were reintroduced after safety improvements, Boeing had launched their 707 aircraft – a better piece of technology. Our early world lead in civil aviation dwindled to nothing and Boeing went on to dominate the industry everywhere.

Similarly BSkyB went straight to satellite broadcast without bothering with the vast capital expenditure which burdened the cable television firms Telewest and NTL, obliged to build out physical networks. Both had to undergo painful restructuring exercises while initial investors and lenders lost billions. And Freeview was born out of the ashes of ITV's doomed ONDigital – despite its pioneering technology. Expensive mistakes were necessary for progress to be made.

The attrition rate of brands and businesses is terrifying. Each entrepreneur has an element of Dr Pangloss about him – irrepressibly optimistic, whatever the circumstances. No start-up would bother if there were too much brutal honesty about the true chances of success. But we should salute the brave chancers who experiment in the hope of a commercial breakthrough. Mostly society is the real winner.

Of course, politicians in their way are the worst chancers of all. They don't accept that the decentralised decision making of the market place is unequivocally superior to central planning. They are addicted to law-making, constant intervention and grand policies. They believe their own promises and manifesto hype, and consistently fail to see that the increase in the role of the state has failed to deliver for citizens. They should realise that most of their initiatives will fail, and that it's our money they are squandering.

April 2005

The Worst Business Decision of All Time

There have been so many financial disasters over the years: the way IBM had Microsoft write an operating system for their personal computer, but let Bill Gates keep all rights to MS-DOS; Lloyd's writing insurance for the American asbestos industry; Nick Leeson sinking Barings Bank with £869 million of unauthorised trading losses; Long Term Capital Management and its $3.5 billion bail out; the $100 billion US savings and loan crisis of the 1980s – and so on and so forth.

But perhaps the stupidest mistake of this bull market is the mass hysteria that gripped major European telecommunications companies in the last couple of years, and persuaded them to bid unprecedented sums for 'Third Generation' or 3G wireless licences. This piece of foolishness has cost at least $100 billion so far and will probably exceed $200 billion by the time the networks are built.

BT, France Telecom, Deutsche Telekom, KPN and Telefonica now have between them a mind-blowing total of 200 billion euros of debt. Thank God BT has less than half the borrowings of France Telecom or Deutsche Telekom. And they haven't even built the infrastructure for the new 3G wireless system. Indeed, there are many who believe the new technology doesn't work. It promises to bring audio, video and high-speed data transmission to mobile handsets, but experts are sceptical about demand and the cost of the new system.

The entire debacle exposes vast hubris on the part of the telecommunications industry, and impressive cunning by government bureaucrats. An ingenious system of blind auctions enabled the various state bodies to maximise the 3G licence fees – perhaps to make up for the super profits the wireless networks had made to date. The seamless technical progression from analogue to digital signal and then to 3G seemed inevitable and a sure-fire thing for the hyper-confident executives of Europe's wireless companies. The promise of emails, live broadcasts and downloadable music files from your mobile seemed irresistible. But the investment, the cost to the consumer and the technological hurdles mean the dream has been shattered. Blinded by science and part of an industry that has only ever known spectacular growth, the management of Europe's major telecom companies have bet an unprecedented sum of money – and lost.

It is now apparent that the projections the various telcos used to justify the massive licence fees are a joke. The dismal flop of WAP has shown that consumers are not really interested in surfing the internet by mobile phone. The public might one day want data, text and images on their handset – but what they really want to do now is simply talk. In Japan trials have revealed major problems with the speed of the service. The European specification, UMTS, is unproven and involves an unprecedented investment in base stations.

The most astonishing aspect of the entire disaster is that for once the civil servants got the better of the capitalists. It is a truism that buying assets from the state is generally a good bet – privatisations often turn out to be real bargains, once the dead hand of the public sector is lifted. And frequently wily entrepreneurs devise ingenious ways of circumventing corporate taxes designed as a levy on scarce resources. But this time the public sector won, and the private sector blew it.

Already several of the bidders who are now suffering the 'winner's curse' are trying to wriggle out. Vivendi, via its mobile operator SFR, last week stalled on a stage payment of $568 million to the French government for its 3G licence. It argued that the material change in business conditions should allow it to renegotiate. Its game of brinkmanship failed however, and by Wednesday it had caved in and paid up. Meanwhile, Sonera, the Finish telecom operator, actually handed back its Norwegian 3G licence and wrote off the 18 million euro investment it had already committed. It has spent 4 billion euros on various 3G licences, and has gone from being one of Scandinavia's most successful companies to one of its most endangered. Dubious analysts are using this surrender as evidence that many 3G licences may be entirely worthless. Never has so much money been willingly given for so little.

Unfortunately this crisis has implications for us all. It means job losses and possible bankruptcies, and a huge transfer of wealth from the private to the public sector – $35 billion in Britain, $46 billion in Germany, and $10 billion in Italy. It means pensions denuded by falling telco shares, while bureaucrats sit on piles of windfall cash. It represents the revenge of the civil servants on some of the gunslingers of the bull market.

October 2001

The Downside of Downsizing

An extraordinary thing started happening on Wall Street in the late 1980s. Large, old-line industrial firms announced enormous restructuring exercises, frequently costing hundreds of millions of dollars – and their shares went up! The stock market loved the idea that tired old conglomerates and inefficient, over-manned companies were willing to cut costs and emphasise shareholder return. Pressure from corporate raiders and buy-out funds made managers and institutional shareholders get tough. One after another, sprawling, traditional organisations in areas like manufacturing cut subsidiaries, staff and overheads to boost margins and their stock prices. A new type of cost-cutting turnaround merchant sprang up to do the painful work. And 'Chainsaw' Al Dunlap was king of these downsizers.

Dunlap had worked in the paper and pulp business, an industry which went through huge turmoil in the 1980s, thanks to overcapacity and the activities of investors like Sir James Goldsmith, who became Dunlap's boss at Crown Zellerbach. By 1996 Dunlap had been involved with seven restructurings, including time at Kerry Packer's Australian media empire. His most financially successful project had been Scott Paper Co., where he became CEO in 1994 and which he sold within 18 months for $9.4 billion to Kimberly-Clark, an uplift since his arrival of 225 per cent. He was seen as ruthless, hands-on and successful. When he was appointed as leader of Sunbeam Corporation, the shares soared 80% in a day.

His havoc-strewn period as boss showed this view to be badly misjudged. Within two years, Dunlap had brought the $1 billion maker of household appliances to its knees. He had leveraged it up with $2.3 billion of debt to make overpriced, second-rate acquisitions, and he had decimated many of Sunbeam's core businesses. Sunbeam lost almost $900 million in 1998, a sum that eliminated the total profits it had made in the five years prior to Dunlap's arrival. The stock had fallen to less than half its level before Dunlap's engagement, and it was mired in shareholder lawsuits and an SEC investigation into its accounting practices. What on earth happened?

The gripping tale of Dunlap's brief reign of terror at Sunbeam in told brilliantly in a new book by John A. Byrne, called *Chainsaw*. It is perhaps the most enjoyable business book I have read this year. But it is not just a saga of a turnaround gone wrong. It is also a dissection of the reality of the 'downsizing' phenomenon, and the philosophy of profit-at-any-price that Wall Street likes. The book is best read alongside Dunlap's own book from 1996, called *Mean Business* – with the subtitle 'How I save bad companies and make good companies great'.

Dunlap appears to be a passionate believer in shareholder value, and was certainly obsessed by the stock price and analyst opinion when serving at Sunbeam. But he demanded the most lavish salary, employment contract and option package ever given to a CEO of a company of Sunbeam's size. He thought that many US corporations were run by lazy, cowardly idiots, but he almost smashed a solid business and needlessly threw thousands of decent workers out of jobs. Dunlap even managed to shaft Michael Price and Ron Perelman, both major Sunbeam shareholders and savvy investors. In his book, Byrne gives detailed examples of how Dunlap was obsessed about announcing cutbacks, even when they were unplanned and probably mistaken. While Sunbeam was not a great company when he took control, the chaos and demoralisation he left behind saw it utterly crippled.

It emerges that the careful restructuring plans which Dunlap boasts about in *Mean Business* were cobbled together entirely by consultants from his pet accounting firm. Frequently these outsiders obtained a completely superficial, hurried idea of a company's strengths and weaknesses, and made proposals based on false assumptions and designed to produce nothing more than bullish press releases. Real turnarounds take time and coordination and are achieved by managers who understand how to motivate employees in difficult circumstances. There is no quick, magic recipe, as Dunlap suggests in his book. Just firing people is not a turnaround.

It also seems that Scott Paper, Dunlap's huge winner, was a company about to collapse when it was bought, thanks to a lack of investment, R&D cutbacks, and a stoppage of maintenance spending. Large scale manufacturing is a long-term business which needs lots of upfront spending and regular investment. Leveraged buyouts have shown how well-invested firms can generate lots of cash for a few years by cutting everything that is not immediate and life-or-death. But profits growth by margin expansion is a short-term game.

The rescue of ailing firms is an important subject. Many of Britain's biggest companies are in need of turning around, including British Airways and Marks & Spencer. No one pretends that reviving ailing businesses is easy or comfortable. But pure slash-and-burn tactics to impress the stock market are not the answer. By learning about Chainsaw Al, at least we can discover how not to do it.

November 1999

GEC a Go-Go

This week venerable GEC paid $4.2 billion net to buy a US business called Fore Systems. Now GEC has been making daring acquisitions since January 1961, when Arnold Weinstock first took control. In the following 35 years he built Britain's largest manufacturing enterprise, mostly buying well, sweating assets, and managing conservatively. It was boring but solid: it missed the fantastic winners that companies like Racal enjoyed with Vodafone, but few big mistakes were made. Now everything is different.

GEC is about to move to the IT sector. Under its thrusting Managing Director Lord Simpson, it is shaking off its reliance on tired industries like defence, and focusing on high growth areas like telecommunications. This all seems eminently sensible in theory. But the problem is that such a transformation does not come cheaply. This latest bold move means GEC has gone into debt for the first time in living memory, despite the £7.7 billion sale of defence businesses to British Aerospace, which was effectively a paper deal.

Fore Systems makes networking equipment like ATM ports, adapter cards and LAN switching ports. It has had an erratic history since it went public in 1995, and in fact net income fell for the year ending 31 March 1998 over the preceding year, and earnings per share in 1999 were below those in 1998 and 1997. Its shares have been a real rollercoaster: in October last year, they traded below $10 – they are now being bought by GEC for $35 each.

By my calculations, GEC is paying goodwill of almost $4 billion. If this is amortised over 20 years, it will mean a charge to the profit and loss statement of $200 million every year for the next 20 years. That means Fore Systems has to almost quadruple its pre-tax profit just to equal the amortisation charge. The statistics of the deal are mind-blowing: a price of over seven times sales, or almost 80 times earnings. The very last sentence of GEC's press release reveals the cost of buying out options belonging to Fore's management: $455 million! I reckon, as a casual observer, it is going to be just a little bit harder to motivate all those boffins in Pittsburgh after such a juicy bonanza like that.

What really is scary is the GEC share price. It has risen almost 8% this week, and helped drive the FTSE 100 to new highs! I suppose the big players in the market are excited about the prospect of GEC joining the internet revolution, and gaining a stratospheric multiple as a consequence, to match the "explosive growth" George Simpson talks about regarding Fore's markets. All this is despite no serious evidence to suggest Fore is really likely to enhance earnings at GEC.

I must be missing something. In my limited experience, large cash acquisitions in the US on very high multiples by large UK companies generally go wrong. The internet/telecoms/networking hardware sector is hot right now, but the pace of change in this industry is lethal. Most successful technology hardware makers have periods of rapid growth, and then face inevitable increased competition and collapsing margins. I note the typical unit sales price of all Fore main product categories fell fairly sharply in both the 1998 and 1999 fiscal years. Fore's sales growth averaged around 25% across the 1998 and 1999 years – and I assume this was boosted by acquisitions. Can this really justify an exit P/E of 79 times?

I expect the smart advisors at Warburg Dillon Read helped GEC reach their decision, with many clever spreadsheets and complex projections. And I am sure GEC employs hundreds of bright fellows who understand switching equipment better than I do. But is this truly the best they could do? Luckily for them, GEC makes over £1 billion a year, so even if Fore proves a failure, the group can withstand it. In March GEC paid around £1.3 billion to buy RELTEC from KKR and others, at another sky-high valuation.

When traditional manufacturers like GEC do deals like this, it is clear that standard measures of investment value and industrial strategy have changed. Unluckily for GEC, it does not enjoy the luxury of keeping all its after-tax earnings (unlike Microsoft, say, which has never paid a dividend) – it is still expected to pay a decent dividend. Its cost of capital must be at least 10% – so how can it realistically expect to make a respectable return with such pricey deals?

On the Motley Fool message board on the internet, one long-standing Fore Systems shareholder wrote of his relief on the deal, and despair with the business: "This company has been a loser for years due to very poor management. They have bungled every acquisition, lost all sales leaders except one...lost all their good technical minds, two founders and so on and so on. Their competition has been outpacing them, and this meant big trouble down the road..." Somehow, I doubt Lord Simpson and his colleagues in GEC's grand new HQ off Bond Street, Mayfair want to hear remarks like that. But they may come back to haunt them.

April 1999

The collapse of GEC/Marconi was one of the most appalling downfalls in British corporate history. From a peak of £12.50 a share and a market value of £35 billion in 2000 there were a series of devastating profit warnings. The company's shares slumped to a low of 1.7p and the whole business teetered close to bankruptcy. The Chairman, Chief Executive and Finance Director all lost their jobs, along with many thousands of blameless, ordinary workers. Subsequently the business has been broken up and sold off in pieces. The advisors who encouraged the whole disaster were nowhere to be seen. The entire tragedy was foreseeable and unnecessary, but hubris, greed and incompetence did for poor old GEC.

Health Clinic

Recent times have seen so many multi-billion pound collapses like Marconi it is easy to miss the smaller disasters. But each one can be a mini-tragedy in its own right, and a truly gruesome experience for all concerned. These corporate implosions are not restricted to the obvious casualty sectors like technology and telecoms: even in private healthcare there have been horror stories.

The most recent such tale is The Health Clinic PLC, an upmarket optician. This business floated on the Full List in July 2000 at 130p. It raised an impressive total of £49 million, of which £30 million was used to pay off debt (partly owed to venture capitalists) and £19 million went straight into the pockets of clever old Dresdner Kleinwort Benson and Sand Aire, the private equity backers of the business. DKB sold its entire holding: Sand Aire retained just 1%. They obviously thought a total valuation of £65 million for nine shops was too rich – after all, the P/E was over 50.

Amazingly, the shares performed: they peaked at 231p last year. Certainly, Health Clinic's ambitions were considerable – it has just 5% of the optical market, dominated by entrenched giants like Boots and Dolland & Aitchison. It boasted of important big company stuff like mission statements and corporate values. It expanded at manic speed into eye laser surgery, and even physiotherapy and dentistry. Its Chief Executive, an ex-Tesco accountant, was reckoned to be an accomplished presenter. He said, "It's not a new business like dotcom". Investors like Gartmore, Hermes and AXA were obviously sold on the project, because they all became major shareholders.

Things started to unravel in late June this year, when the preliminary results to 30 April 2002 were delayed pending the "resolution of certain non-cash accounting issues". The shares rapidly weakened from 142p to 75p, although the fall was stabilised by the publication of the results on 1st July. They announced that the company had grown to 20 clinics and had revenues of £32 million – but achieved operating profits of just £100,000 following £3.3 million of one-off charges.

More sinister was the increase in debt: borrowings had climbed from £4.6 million the previous year to an astounding £23.3 million – up from £14 million at the interim stage. The company had experienced a cash outflow of £18.5 million for the year. But the statement ended by saying: "We remain confident and optimistic for the future" and insisted "four new clinics are planned" and "funding remains in place for this expansion." Meanwhile the Finance Director stepped down. The shares bounced to 95p.

Another bombshell detonated ten days ago. On the 23rd of August, the Friday before the Bank Holiday, Health Clinic put out an opaque statement suggesting the company faced a funding crisis. The new interim Finance Director had noticed a £3 million working capital shortfall, and the bank was insisting on more equity since the projections were wrong. The capital expenditure programme of a few weeks before had been halted and the April 2002 report and accounts were to be delayed. A few big shareholders were being told they would have to stump up more cash. All this is very different news from June's "non-cash" accounting issues.

This grim announcement sent the shares into freefall. Today they stand at around 17p – not much more than 10% of their issue price – after millions were unloaded this week. The Chairman, Alan Smith, must feel he's had an unlucky year. He is also Chairman of the ill-fated Mothercare, and a non-executive Director of The Big Food Group. Lord MacLaurin of Knebworth is also a non-executive Director and must similarly find the whole thing tiresome, although the value destruction at Health Clinic pales into insignificance next to the £50 billion of shareholder wealth lost this year by Vodafone – where MacLaurin is Chairman.

Rebuilding credibility for the business will now be an uphill struggle, especially since 40% of the staff took shares in the placing. There must be question marks over the management and the business concept. I wish them all the best of luck. I should declare an interest here: I'm a founder of another dental business, but I don't think we really compete. I've written about Health Clinic not to rubbish a rival but because I follow the sector, and know it's no pushover making money in for-profit health services. These are dangerous times for investors, where problems can occur even in what appear to be 'safe-haven' industries. As Ted Turner said, "It ain't as easy as it looks."

August 2002

Sadly for shareholders, the business failed and was liquidated in December 2004.

Cammell Laird – A Marine Tragedy

Cammell Laird has a proud history in shipbuilding. It commenced making sea vessels in 1824, and since then over 5,000 ships have been built in its yards. It has gone through a number of reorganisations and changes in ownership over the last 177 years, but since re-emerging as a public company in July 1997 it has expanded dramatically. The dream was to reverse the decline in Britain's shipbuilding industry, which has slumped from 38% of world tonnage in 1950 to 1% today.

Now sadly this vision of a world-beating British shipbuilder has been dashed. PriceWaterhouseCoopers were appointed receivers to Cammell Laird's subsidiaries a couple of weeks ago. The company's sudden and horrifying collapse has left employees, shareholders and bondholders stunned. How can a company slide from a market value of over £300 million to insolvency in just six months? The causes of this unhappy disaster are the combination of a dispute with an Italian customer, wildly over-ambitious management and gullible advisors, investors and lenders.

In truth shipbuilding and repair is a tough industry characterised by low margins, lumpy orders, frequent cyclical downturns, high working capital needs, subsidized overseas competition and a history of insolvency. European yards have been cemeteries for investors for decades, since low-cost competition from South Koreans and others has driven work to Asia. The amazing seven-fold climb of Cammell Laird's share price in four years from an adjusted 20p to over 140p always looked overdone.

The risks seem obvious in hindsight. Not only was Cammell Laird in a difficult business: it expanded by acquisition at an extraordinary pace in a number of different territories, and did so on a relatively small equity base. It funded the bulk of this growth through an amazing junk bond issue launched in just October last year for 125 million euros – at the exorbitant coupon of 12%. It is baffling as to how DLJ got the funding away, and why Merrill

Lynch and Standard & Poor's were willing to rate the bonds. The bonds can only ever have made one quarterly interest payment – if that. One assumes there will be ferocious litigation against various advisors from furious bondholders, who I imagine will get a fraction of the face value of their debt back as is normally the case in such workouts.

Following the bond issue the company was 90% geared, and it had very recently taken on several bold new projects. These included the purchase in July last year of "one of the largest repair docks in the world" in Marseille, France's biggest port, as well as 49% of Cascade General, the largest West Coast ship repair business based in Portland, Oregon. This owns the "largest floating repair dock in the Americas". Overall these purchases gave the company "shipyards spanning the Western hemisphere". While these phrases were impressive, none of Cammell Laird's acquisitions ever seem to have made any profits. Previously it had rescued Bulgaria's insolvent Varna shipyard, which had owed $77 million – as well as buying Gibraltar's repair docks. It had also bought the Camper & Nicholson luxury yacht maker and two offshore support vessels, and even its own cruise ship. Making that lot pay would have taken management of genius.

In among all this excitement Cammell Laird announced a contract worth 83 million euros to refit a liner for Costa Crociere SpA, an Italian cruise line. This was the deal which actually brought the edifice down. Although based in Genoa, Costa Crociere is actually owned by Carnival Corporation from Miami – and was once 50% owned by UK-based Airtours. A dispute flared up in November last year while the 'Costa Classica' was en-route to Britain. The liner promptly turned around, dumped 30 Cammell Laird staff in Northern Spain and refused to honour any payments for the considerable amount of work already done. Unfortunately the contract was back-end loaded.

Within weeks, John Stafford, a 24% shareholder and the Chief Executive of Cammell Laird had resigned and the shares went into a tailspin from which they never recovered. Hopes of a huge $500 million order for new liners from a US start-up called "Luxus" came to nothing. No trading figures have been announced since July last year: the last published statements showed sales of £139 million and pre-tax profits of nearly £16 million. So despite the company's apparent profitability and "enquiries totalling £750 million", it ran out of cash within nine months. The last balance sheet had debt of £47 million – yet the company received nearly £80 million of cash from the bond offering three months later and still went bust. I suspect the company had no assets which actually generated cash – and plenty which absorbed it.

The tale is a tangled one and will run on for a while. The receivers are pursuing litigation against Costa Crociere, and Trade and Industry secretary Stephen Byers has apparently told them not to sell the yards in Merseyside, Teeside and Tyneside to "asset strippers", for fear of endangering some of the 3,000 jobs at stake worldwide. The whole bizarre fiasco must be awkward for Beeson Gregory, who advised on a placing in August last year at 105p a share. The Directors meanwhile blamed among other things "employee morale" for the demise of the business. One hopes the Board's morale is boosted by the fact that they sold over £11 million worth of shares in 1999.

April 2001

The Software Industry Rip-Off

In the outcry about "rip-off Britain", no-one has mentioned the industry which provides perhaps the worst value of all – the computer software industry. It is no coincidence that Microsoft is the world's most profitable company, and enjoys net margins of over 40% – a return which would be inconceivable in any other trade. Consumers and business pay excessive mark-ups for software, yet the products they buy are full of flaws. We are approaching the Millennium with trepidation, because software companies sold everyone products which may have Y2K defects. Users have had to spend hundreds of millions fixing the possible Y2K bugs – and the software suppliers have benefited. Across the world, we tolerate extortionate prices and shoddy products from software companies, blind to the poor value they offer. Why on earth is this?

We put up with faulty, overpriced products because we do not understand what we are buying, and because we have been fooled into thinking we need more complex products than we do, and because software companies launch products before they are ready. The very nature and history of the computer software industry has perpetuated this giant con job.

Like many technology industries, the software industry developed in the US. And the worldwide software trade is still dominated by Americans – 18 of the top 20 software companies are US, and 75% of the pre-packaged software is US made. Companies like Microsoft, Oracle and Novell were able to write and test programmes and build large businesses in their massive home market, and so could export and dominate overseas markets having already expensed supposedly finished products.

These software companies have fantastic valuations, because they have a hugely profitable business model. They originate a product which costs almost nothing to replicate and produce once the initial investment is repaid. They regularly sell products which crash and have defects – or 'bugs', a much less honest word invented by the software industry. They try to capture customers by selling them imperfect products which require ongoing 'upgrades' – a software industry euphemism for corrections. Customers become prisoners to a particular supplier and invariably have little recourse to law, thanks to one-sided and obscure software licence agreements.

Whenever a firm announces it is undertaking a major software installation, beware. How many such projects happen on time and on budget, without breakdowns or cost overruns? I am aware of a retailer which has recently written off its entire investment in an electronic point of sale system which was less than two years old. The system never worked properly and failed to provide the information promised. The write-off represented more than an entire year's profits. Such events are not uncommon when talking about software – quality and reliability standards are not seen as priorities by suppliers.

Because few people understand the technical detail of computer software, suppliers can bamboozle customers into thinking they need a more sophisticated and expensive product than they really do. Software companies are also able to blame users for problems with the software when the product itself was poorly designed or adapted. Software products are routinely over-engineered with useless add-ons so that suppliers can claim more benefits and charge more. Even more outrageously, software companies churn out new releases and force companies to switch by withdrawing support for old versions. The software guru who orders the software within a customer firm wants his budget to be big to increase his importance and pay.

The greatest software rip-off is the illusion that software needs replacing or improving every three years or so – the built-in obsolescence. The argument is always that such upgrades will improve productivity and help the client make more profit. In fact customers mostly do not use new features, which are anyway often untested and capable of corrupting existing data. Firms end up with dozens of different, incompatible versions of software and have to spend vast amounts more transferring files, enabling software to work together, or end up having to throw everything away and start from scratch. Companies are never reminded of the disruption, data risks, downtime and distraction of training and all the other drawbacks when being sold new software features.

Britain suffers a substantial trade deficit with the US in software, as do virtually all countries. The American software industry is an important employer and the largest contributor to the balance of trade there. But complacent and ruthless software companies are endangering their own industry by neglecting quality and value. Countries like India will catch up with California and undercut the US unless the latter stop producing software that is "good enough" and start selling something more robust. Free software like Linux will supplant other systems unless they offer better value.

Instead of concentrating purely on things like overpriced cars, the government should start getting excited on the public's behalf about being ripped off by software companies. Those software suppliers might then focus on working with their customers, rather than on exploiting them.

November 2003

Frank Timis

Sometimes there are unexploded bombs waiting to detonate in the nether regions of the stock market that are so obvious you wonder how bright investors get blown up. One of these booby traps was Regal Petroleum, the £400 million stock whose shares plunged 60% in one day recently.

It really was a surprise that sophisticated institutions like Commerzbank, Henderson, Fidelity and Artemis all held declarable stakes in Regal. The facts were there for anyone to see. For example, there is the matter of the Executive Chairman, Frank Vasile Timis, a colourful Romanian mining entrepreneur and principal driving force behind Regal. Can the above fund managers concerned really have failed to notice that Mr Timis was charged with possession of heroin with intent to sell in Australia not once, but twice in both 1990 and 1994? Did they not check on the progress of his first great Romanian gold play, Gabriel Resources? The shares of this Canadian company have caved in by over 70% this year alone. This is a company upon which much of Mr Timis' early reputation was founded. It has not proved much of an investment.

Mr Timis does not like to restrict his activities to simply serving as main promoter of the grandly named Regal. Until May 2003 he was in addition Chairman, Chief Executive Officer and President of European Goldfields, also quoted on AIM and again advised by Evolution and focused on natural resource extraction in the Balkans. These shares have also fallen, from 135p earlier this year to 79p, valuing it at £92 million. Curiously, Commerzbank are also a large shareholder in this stock. Like Regal, this company loses money and seems to suffer a revolving door to the boardroom.

Although he stepped down from the board, Mr Timis retains a 20% stake in European Goldfields. He obtained much of this by turning a mining asset to the public company at a sizeable profit within 5 months of his investment. This was his 21% stake in the

Hellas mine, which he sold to European Goldfields for £24 million in cash and 18 million shares worth £24 million at the time. Evolution kindly raised the £40 million cash required for the transaction in October last year. Mr Timis had paid just £12 million for his Hellas stake – so he created a 300% personal profit of £30 million in under 6 months.

During this period a helpful report was published by Behre Dolbear, a mining consultancy, which suggested the Hellas deposit was actually worth $500 million – even though it was sold by the Greek government for just 11 million euros less than 9 months before. This 'valuation' apparently justified the four-fold uplift in value. Given that European Goldfields also participated in the initial Hellas investment with Timis and that he was a related party, it is staggering that he was permitted to take out such a huge amount of cash in the deal – seemingly approved by advisors and Directors and supported by eager institutional lemmings – sorry, investors.

In February, another speculative mining play was unleashed from the Timis stable. This was Sierra Leone Diamond Company, which raised £20 million at 75p and was valued at £72 million on flotation. Three months' later its shares lie slumped at 39p. Yet again, the vehicle is registered somewhere obscure – this time Bermuda, while the mining deposits are in war-torn Africa rather than Central Europe. As ever, the company announcements and broker's reports are full of complex and highly technical details about the prospects for finding riches in the earth. I'm impressed investors thought they understood enough of this arcane stuff to risk their money. But their analysis of management competence and reliability seems curiously superficial.

According to media reports, Mr Timis blames hedge funds for short selling Regal's shares and over-reacting to bad news. I haven't talked to these sinister bear raiders, but I suspect the collapse in Mr Timis' reputation and his share prices is simply the City coming to its senses.

May 2005

5

Economics

A Philosophy of Capitalism

It seems odd that there are so few intellectual works which deal with the philosophy of capitalism. There are millions of words written annually on the mechanics of business, but virtually none on the ultimate purpose of it all. Where is the metaphysical justification for the toil and effort? Is the rat race an exercise in futility? In the last hundred years it has become the dominant creed almost everywhere, replacing religion, Marxism and the like – yet there are almost no texts that rationalize why men strive so hard to build enterprises.

Why is it important for those engaged in accumulating wealth to think about the deeper principles underlying their daily work? Why trouble themselves about the ethics of their acquisitive urges? I think an understanding of their motivations, and the meaning of our economic and social systems, helps expand the mind and gives a sense of moral value. This is altogether more profound than Adam Smith's cynical view that "The chief enjoyment of riches consists in the parade of riches."

Perhaps business is a subconscious attempt to create something immortal, and in so doing, deny death – even if, as Thomas Gay said: "The paths of glory lead but to the grave." There is no doubt that many successful firms outlive their founders. A few empire-builders consciously plan to leave a commercial legacy, and be remembered. After all, a dynamic, noisy thing like an active business is far more powerful a reminder than most memorials.

There have been various attempts to explain the spiritual side of business, showing that "economic self-assertion" was a "moral obligation". Benjamin Franklin, in his *Autobiography* and *The Way to Wealth*, expounded the classic case study of the Puritan-Protestant work ethic, when he observed "the way to wealth, if you desire it, is as plain as the way to market. It depends chiefly on two words, industry and frugality." He believed that religion demanded success, and that capitalist advancement was a way to serve God. As quoted in Proverbs, 22:29: "Seest thou a man diligent in his business? He shall stand before kings." Making money was a natural vocation: the profit motive was a force for good – God and Mammon stood shoulder to shoulder.

Of course the Scottish economist Adam Smith was a formidable proponent of capitalism. His epic work, *An Enquiry into the Nature and Cause of The Wealth of Nations,* published in 1776, introduced the concept of the 'invisible hand' that drives an entrepreneur to benefit society as a by-product of his own self interest. "He intends only his own gain, and he is, in this, as in many other cases, led by an invisible hand to promote an end which was no part of his intention." His moral insight about the world of trading has never been surpassed: he saw that "by mutual consent and to mutual advantage" men will exchange goods and skills and enrich themselves, given sufficient freedom and adequate property rights.

The Victorian Samuel Smiles, in his management classic *Self-Help,* celebrates the achievements of individuals who advanced society through their industry. Inventors, manufacturers, merchants, scientists – all were praised for their energy, courage, and willpower. He believed entrepreneurs possessed "prudence, forethought and self-denial – the true basis of manly character." He saw a reasonable level of wealth creation as honourable, but hoarding of large sums as "characteristic of the narrow-souled and the miserly."

Ayn Rand, authoress of *The Fountainhead* and inventor of objectivism, was perhaps the foremost exponent of the unfettered philosophy of laissez-faire capitalism. She originated "the concept of man as a heroic being" with "productive achievement as his noblest activity." Her books and beliefs are still remarkably popular today, especially in the USA. Indeed, Eddie Lampert, the wunderkind behind the recent mega-merger of retailers Sears and Kmart, is apparently an advocate. I like the idea of an entrepreneur who has the time and discipline to study a 1,000 page tome like *Atlas Shrugged*, perhaps Rand's most romantic work.

The Austrian school of economists were also philosophers of a sort. They tended to have a powerful faith in entrepreneurs and free enterprise. The three greatest contributors to their body of work have been Ludwig von Mises, with *Human Action*, Friedrich von Hayek, with *The Road to Serfdom*, and Joseph Schumpeter, with *Capitalism, Socialism and Democracy*. They were libertarians and free marketers, who celebrated the 'creative destruction' of capitalism as a source of endless renewal and inventiveness.

More recently, biologists have analysed the natural history of successful people and compared it to studies of primate behaviour. They suggest the driving forces behind ambitious capitalists are similar to those in alpha apes: a desire to control resources, social dominance and effective display. All these strategies are aimed at ensuring a winning future for one's genes. The result is the survival of the fittest – or perhaps just the richest. This hardly sounds a very cerebral answer to the conundrum of capitalism – but a fairly compelling explanation nevertheless.

December 2004

China

They say that four in the morning is the suicide hour. Last week I was on the 75th floor of a skyscraper hotel in Shanghai at 4am, suffering from jetlag, looking down at the adjacent building site. There I saw a frenzy of industrious welders lighting up the night, constructing another giant building, part of the miracle of modern China. The labourers were working seven days a week, 24 hours a day – at less than $5 a day. And then I knew, more than ever, that unless we change, they will in time lay the decadent West to waste.

I came home to a new ruling against Britain's opt out from the Working Time Directive from Strasbourg, supported by Labour MEPs. This insists no-one in Britain can work more than 48 hours a week – even if they want to. It was a stark demonstration of the deep stupidity of the goons at the TUC, and the circus clowns of the European Parliament. None of these buffoons work in the private sector – none of them produce anything except strikes and bad law – none of them have risked their capital to build a business or ever created a real job. They are in profound denial about the grim realities of the global marketplace and Britain's serious vulnerabilities as a first world economy.

China and India already represent 40% of the world's population. They are both growing very rapidly and are super-competitive – across services as well as manufacturing. In the years ahead, which exactly are the industries left where Britain will still compete? Hamstrung by preposterous regulations, high taxes, a burdensome welfare system, and anti-business legislation – how on earth are we to retain our standard of living? I do wish the fools in Westminster and Brussels would offer some practical solutions, rather than more bureaucracy and costs. Instead union leaders talk about restrictive new legislation as a "victory for commonsense".

New Labour has enjoyed a benign period in office while global interest rates have hovered at 50 year lows. Investors have tolerated reduced returns and consumers have borrowed to fund spending. The government has expanded the state recklessly to prop up the economy and buy votes – going into hock in the process. But inevitably principal has to be repaid. The consumer is knackered, unemployment is rising, sterling is on the slide, and personal and state deficits are climbing. Meanwhile, the politicians fiddle while Rome burns, cosily insulated from the real world within their ministerial cars and gold-plated pensions.

It is important to see China in action first hand to realise what a formidable player it has become. Its economy has grown at a rate of two to three times ours for at least fifteen years. It has lifted 250 million people out of poverty during that period. There has never been an economic transformation like it. On more or less every level, China can offer world-class quality at a fraction of the cost of a rival in Europe. And yet rather than unshackle entrepreneurs, the Luddites in the EU are attempting to further undermine our ability to fend off the onslaught. As an example, exports of certain textiles to the EU from China have risen by over 500% this year alone after the ending of quotas. The political classes across France, Germany – and even Britain – have lost the plot. They imagine the EU nations can retain their share of world markets and global power while indulging in welfare systems that undermine ambition and discourage effort.

Part of the reason politicians and civil servants fail to govern honestly is that they abuse language relentlessly. They employ words like 'fair' and 'poverty' when no-one can agree what they mean. They describe huge increases in salaries for public sector workers as 'investment'. They say they have not increased income tax – and yet they raise national insurance – which in the real world is the same thing. Our leaders specialise in humbug and ostrich-like behaviour. When will they wake up?

Like companies going broke, countries slide into recession first slowly – then violently quickly. This time it may be rather harder to pull ourselves out of the mire. It seems horribly apparent where we are now. The misguided policies of the last few years are having their inevitably damaging effect, and the economy is clearly spluttering. I have rarely seen such a sudden fall in business confidence as has occurred in the last few months. Government and consumer finances are ill-equipped to deal with a sharp downturn. I recommend *Sunday Telegraph* readers prepare themselves for a rough ride.

May 2005

The Importance of Title

The headline here does not refer to an honour such as a knighthood granted by the Queen. Rather, it describes the legal ownership of property. And when I say property, I do not just mean buildings and land – I mean any bundle of rights in a legal sense.

So the property might be real or it could be intangible, such as patents, licences, franchises or copyrights. The issue of ownership and title to property is a major reason why the Western world has made economic progress and why developing countries struggle to get richer.

The ability to clearly possess and exploit property, and to transfer it, remains the bedrock of capitalism and without it, societies stay on the fringe. Ever since The Bill of Rights in 1689, British subjects have been entitled to own private property. Yet this basic right is to all intents not available in many countries.

It is estimated that only 25 of the world's 207 nations have a contractual basis for property matters. The rest have limited legal rights and enforceability. This creates havoc, and leads to waste and immiseration.

In countries where ownership is uncertain, assets cannot be used to raise debt. Lenders will not extend credit if clean title to land cannot be obtained, because their security will be impaired – so improvement cannot take place because mortgages are unavailable.

In both the Philippines and Peru, less than 50 per cent of urban property is legitimately titled – in Egypt, less than 10 per cent has clear title! All over the Third World, large proportions of the population are the equivalent of squatters: always at risk of eviction or having their property seized. In such shifting circumstances, long-term enterprise is impossible.

Thanks to these unreliable systems of property ownership, there is mis-allocation of resources and gross inefficiency. Capital cannot be freed and made available for investment, because assets cannot be leveraged. Where planning laws are uncertain and administration corrupt, material progress is slow and many operate in the black economy.

This means they do not invest because they are unsure they have real possession of assets, and they do not pay taxes because they are outside the law. Everything is temporary and short term; credit is unavailable and a cash-only system prevails. In such a society there is little incentive or opportunity to invest or save. Hence such countries remain unproductive and undeveloped. Modern civilisation develops where settled people cultivate land.

Of course, the clearest examples of places where private property rights do not exist are in communist states. In pathetically impoverished countries such as Cuba or North Korea, individuals are discouraged from owning and improving land.

The wholesale collapse of Soviet Russia in the 1980s proved that the Marxist system of property rights did not work. Individuals will only really apply effort and enrich themselves if they enjoy secure property rights. China is a contradiction. It is still nominally a communist regime, but privatisation has proceeded at a rapid pace in recent years. Economic growth has been remarkable, thanks to the restoration of de facto private property rights – yet within a Marxist state. Its huge populations and proximity to such Asian powerhouses as Singapore, Taiwan and, of course, Hong Kong have enabled China to embrace a form of capitalism without granting real democracy to its people.

Complaints from foreign investors regarding the fickleness of the rule of law mean the system still has deep flaws, as far as business is concerned. But China has nevertheless made extraordinary progress in a short time. Yet it fails to respect intellectual property, and is a world centre of piracy in fake goods such as counterfeit cigarettes, clothing and CDs.

The British legal system of property ownership is cumbersome but reasonably effective. It stands in stark contrast to the chaos in so many Third World countries. When your lawyer tells you the title to your house is clean, it means more than we perhaps realise. We do not appreciate how lucky we are to be able to truly say that we own our own homes.

June 2000

Russia

Occasionally I write an article that damages my business career, or attracts the threat of a libel writ, but this week I'm going one better. I'm tackling a subject that might get me murdered, because it is simply too fascinating to resist. The topic? Russia and its robber barons.

I spent last weekend in St Petersburg, my first time in the Russian Republic for five years. On my previous visit to Moscow, I spent twenty minutes pinned to the floor of a nightclub by gunmen in flak jackets and balaclavas. They were actually police, searching for Chechen gangsters, but at the time I thought all the customers were about to be robbed. On the surface things have improved since then – despite the summer 1998 ruble devaluation, debt default and loan moratorium. There are many more smart foreign cars, flashy shops and prosperous locals in expensive restaurants. Yet outside the major cities, Russia remains a huge country of stark contrasts. In the provinces, life is rudimentary and mostly agrarian, but in the capital some of the world's wealthiest tycoons have made fortunes through wholesale theft.

The classic story is that of Mikhail Khodorkovsky, controlling shareholder and Chief Executive of Yukos Oil, Russia's second largest oil company. In just seven years he has manipulated his way to a fortune of perhaps $4 billion and become the country's richest man at the age of 38. Russia is the world's second largest oil exporter, and thanks to the revival of the oil price in the last couple of years, Yukos earned around $3.7 billion on $7.3 billion in 2001: its market capitalisation is around $15 billion. Khodorkovsky and his partners probably own over 60% of the business.

The Yukos boss started his fortune by forming a bank called Menatep. Its principal client was the federal government of Boris Yeltsin. It handled the sale of Russian state assets in 1995, when the bankrupt government was in desperate need of funds to pay bills. A preposterous loans-for-shares auction took place –

perhaps the largest organised fraud of modern times. Amazingly, Khordorkovsky was able to buy almost 80% of Yukos for $350 million – probably using the government's own money in the process – and perhaps even the resources of Yukos itself. To put this in perspective, Yukos recently paid an interim DIVIDEND of $300 million.

Later the entrepreneurial Russian had a run-in with Kenneth Dart, a Western magnate who had minority stakes in two core Yukos subsidiaries. But Khordorkovsky had majority control, and so he transferred all the value out – according to Dart, "illegally looting the partially owned subsidiaries." Eventually Dart settled for an undisclosed amount, probably bullied by the ruthless Russian who held all the cards.

In 1997, Yukos borrowed hundreds of millions of dollars from banks like WestLB, Daiwa, Standard Chartered, CSFB and so forth, to make acquisitions. When the Russian financial system collapsed, virtually all its banks defaulted on their loans, including Bank Menatep, the effective borrower. The Western lenders took ownership of their collateral – 29% of Yukos' shares – held as security for their $266 million of debt.

The management of Yukos then moved into action and threatened to drown the banks' equity with vast new share issues to obscure offshore holders – who would pay for the stock in IOUs. The company's spokesman said: "This was a normal defensive manoeuvre." Meanwhile the prize assets of Yukos were being sold for peanuts to unknown overseas companies. The Western banks caved in and sold their shares for perhaps $125 million – perhaps a twentieth of their current value – back to the Khordorkovsky camp.

These days Russian President Vladimir Putin is close friends with President Bush and an ally in the war on terrorism. The Russians are coming in from the cold again. There are fewer stories about mafia killings on the streets of Moscow. Their economy and stock market have staged extraordinary recoveries, and the currency is stable. Meanwhile 10% of the shares in Yukos are owned in ADR form and it publishes its accounts according to US GAAP. It boasts of high corporate governance standards and several foreign Directors sit on its 15-member board. But investors and lenders to the company should study its history and the ethics of its Chief Executive before deciding to get involved. Leopards tend not to change their spots. All those who carry on regardless deserve everything they get.

June 2002

Khodorkovsky fell foul of Russian premier Vladimir Putin and was jailed for fraud and tax evasion for nine years in May 2005. Meanwhile, Yukos was broken up by the Russian government and declared bankrupt in August 2006.

Student Misery

This is a grim time to be a new graduate. There were certainly challenges when I left university in 1983, but these were as nothing compared to the difficulties today's students face. I do not envy them.

One shocking statistic struck me recently. The average age of the first time home buyer in Britain has now risen to 35. I bought my first property when I was 23 in the mid 1980s – which was a fairly typical age for the first-time buyer then. During the intervening 20 odd years Britain seems to have adopted the Italian model, where children often stay with their parents until they enter their 30s. They tend only to buy a home when they marry and have a family. Perhaps the phenomenon of the late starter contributes to the desperately low birth rates in Northern Italy, despite its evident prosperity and the dominance of the Catholic Church.

People here are buying homes much later because of the soaring price of property – and because students now graduate with so much debt. Barclays recently published a survey showing students now typically owe over £12,000 to the government, banks and credit card companies. This amount has ballooned from just over £2,000 in 1994. When I graduated some students left university with modest debts, but basically banks would only lend students an overdraft of a few hundred pounds, and grants funded their undergraduate courses, so the opportunity to become overextended was limited.

It isn't just a place to live that's become too expensive. I bought a car the year I graduated and have owned one ever since. But thanks to rising claims, the typical annual insurance premium for a 21 year old driver in London is now £2,000 – meaning most graduates cannot afford to drive, or at least drive legally.

The state has partly funded the vast expansion in higher education by forcing recipients to pay for their learning. Since a degree is thought to be a sound investment, borrowing to pay for tuition makes sense – especially in an era of low interest rates. There are now two million full-time students. The government's stated policy is to ensure half of all 18 year olds study for a degree by 2010. Of course, more does not necessarily mean better; many employers believe degrees have become debased by the huge growth in university places. There must be serious doubt about the practical value some students receive – especially since they give up at least three years of work in order to study.

Moreover, there are serious questions over the mix of qualifications being obtained. In total 23% of all graduating students want to work in media or marketing. I should think the true demand for such graduates is a tenth of that. Yet there are desperate shortages of pharmacists, dentists, chefs, plumbers and the like. We are producing thousands of graduates with unrealistic expectations and irrelevant qualifications. Can it be a surprise that the number of graduates expecting to get a job straight away is at a ten year low, or that the number applying for post-graduate study is at an all-time high?

Again we seem to be copying other countries like Germany or America, where young people join the workforce much later – often at 25 or 26. Perhaps with greater life expectancy and later retirement ages, it makes sense to delay one's career. Could this become a lost generation, without a stake in society, never growing up: without their own homes, cars and in jobs for which they're overqualified?

To improve matters there are a number of changes to policy that should be made. More places for useful qualifications in areas like nursing, pharmacy, medicine, IT and so forth should be created, with the funding being diverted from the non-vocational liberal arts. Students should be strongly encouraged to get part-time work while studying to keep their debts under control. Inheritance tax rates should be slashed – especially for family homes – to enable parents to pass their houses to their children without the taxman taking 40% and so forcing a sale.

March 2005

Japan Will Recover

I have just spent a week in Tokyo, and it was an educational experience. The Japanese have been somewhat humbled by their present economic woes, but their inherent strengths continue to impress. Their economy may be contracting by an annualised rate of 5.3%, yet they remain the second financial superpower. Many in the West are taking delight in the collapse of the yen, Tokyo property prices, the Japanese banking sector and the Nikkei 225 Index. Do not, however, write Japan off – they will come back, and probably stronger and more competitive than ever.

Moreover, their troubles will hardly improve matters here. It is inconceivable that Europe and America can escape unscathed from the Asian crisis. Not only are Western exporters hit by reduced Asian demand for their goods, but South East Asia is now exporting here for its life. With massive underutilized capacity and hugely more competitive currencies, their products are now unbeatable value. The ballooning US trade deficit is the proof. So world growth this year is now likely to be less than 2%, and a sharp slowdown probable here.

The other principal reason why we should not gloat is that the Japanese people are resilient and industrious. They rebuilt their nation into a formidable capitalist state after their industries were levelled by WWII, despite having minimal natural resources and an inhospitable and cramped land-mass. They are now dominant in a huge range of industries – electrical and electronic appliances, machine tools, motorbikes, industrial robots and shipbuilding, to name but a few categories. Japan did not achieve this manufacturing supremacy by luck, but by application, education, investment and discipline.

These traits and beliefs remain. While the Japanese business model of market share at all costs is flawed, it is by no means totally redundant. Japanese society is still remarkably homogenous and safe and the Japanese hell-bent on improving their lot. Their ability to save and innovate is astounding. Over a third of all Japanese attend university – and most study technical and practical subjects, rather than liberal arts waffle. Research and development spending as a percentage of GNP is around 50% higher than in the UK or USA; they register almost twice as many patents annually in the US than Germany and Britain combined.

The Japanese are relentless capitalists. Just look at the way a company like Fuji has steadily eroded Kodak's US market share of photographic film, while retaining its home market. Kodak invented modern photography and enjoyed a virtual world monopoly – it is now seen as weak and fumbling. Remember how Nintendo, Sega and now Sony shook the world's toy market upside down, and how Hasbro and Mattel are still struggling to catch up. Observe the continued slide of General Motors and the encroachment of Toyota. Once the Japanese turn their attention to the service industries of the world, we should prepare for an onslaught.

The Japanese government say they are committed to structural reform and deregulation. They had better mean it this time. They have promised to reduce personal and corporate tax rates, and shake up the banking and insurance fields, as well as crank up infrastructure spending. They have already opened up the securities industry. The key is to reorganise the bloated local and central government bureaucracies which are stifling progress and change. They must permit more cross-border M&A activity, and encourage shareholder orientated restructuring. And they must forget the ideal of permanent full employment – they suffer a much lower labour productivity than most OECD members. Nevertheless, they can afford to see unemployment rise by 50% and still be way below the developed nations' average. The country needs to prepare for a rapidly ageing population and China's ascendance.

If carried through, these improvements will reinvigorate Japan and make her more dynamic and efficient. Her resilient and productive workers will emerge from the bubble economy of the late 1980s chastened and tougher. They have been suffering a hangover since 1990. My view is that now is that most painful, final spasm before things start to get gradually better. One should remember that Japan has experienced wild economic swings before and prospered – they cut costs during the mid 1980s when the yen appreciated against the dollar and kept their edge. I suspect the present Japanese mess revolves around finance and property, rather than profound defects in their technology or attitude.

Japan continues to enjoy the highest per capita national income of any major nation, and their even distribution of wealth is a huge strength. They are more adaptable than we like to think. They have entirely re-invented themselves in the last 40 years, and yet have retained the feel of an ancient race. While the Pacific Century may have been deferred, Japan is superbly positioned to grow with the Asian Tiger economies when they rebound. Its success is the classic example of how strength of purpose and diligence are what build nations, not physical advantages.

April 2004

The Age of the Dumpies is Dawning

Two new books examine the rapid ageing of the Western population and how it will affect business and society. Both make fascinating reading – the American version is *Gray Dawn* by Peter Peterson (Time Books); the British equivalent is *Agequake* by Paul Wallace (Nicholas Brealey Publishing). The latter is perhaps more relevant to us since the demographics and economics of each country are different. Nevertheless, Peterson's book is more authoritative and considerably more scary.

Over the centuries many forecasts have warned of a crisis of overpopulation, which has not really happened. But as a society we are getting steadily older. In the next 20 years the proportion of the UK population under 35 will fall sharply while the percentage aged over 35 will climb. This will have a significant impact on business, finance and society.

Viagra had the fastest launch of any drug. Pfizer enjoyed such a huge boom because it is cashing in on an ageing population that wishes to retain its vigour. It shows how healthcare spending will take a larger share of gross domestic product as we get older. Health expenditure for people older than 65 is four times higher than it is for the rest of us.

For patient investors, buying shares in drug and healthcare companies makes sense. Other sectors to look for opportunities include travel firms and leisure businesses, since this generation is happier spending their wealth rather than leaving it to their children. And builders of retirement communities look attractive. Overall every investment portfolio should take account of the demographic changes facing society and adjust accordingly.

In the UK, households headed by 50 to 64 year olds spend almost a third more than all the other households on holidays. The number taken by those over 55 rose by a third in the first half of the 1990s. They are big buyers of cruise and mini breaks: tour operators and travel firms should benefit from these changing demographics.

Relative to many wealthier countries, demographic shifts will favour Britain. Japan and Germany in particularly have rapidly ageing populations, and dramatically underfunded pensions systems. In Britain we have a mixed state and private pension system, and our pension funds have heavily invested in equities: in 1996 our pension fund assets as a percentage of GDP were more than 70 per cent, against less than 10 per cent in Germany, France and Italy.

Worse still, public retirement benefits in these countries are far more lavish than in the UK, which may lead to more unsustainable burden on future working generations. Moreover, we have a less rapidly ageing population than many other European countries, save Ireland. In 2010, Ireland will have one person over 65 or older for every five people of working age, while Germany will have one in three. This helps explain the country's recent renaissance as a Celtic tiger economy.

By 2030 Britain's state spending on pensions and healthcare is predicted to rise from today's 10.5 per cent of GDP to 15.5 per cent. Although this is alarming, it will be the lowest percentage among the G7 nations. We also retire later than most, which means we carry on being productive until later in life and less of a burden on social security. As Peterson says: "The money it saves on doctors, together with it's radical pension reform, distinguishes Britain as better situated than any nation to weather the global ageing storm." We have either been lucky or clever, and may have a more secure future than most, assuming we do not allow our colleagues in Europe to replenish their pension deficit with our funds. God forbid we should go from being Yuppies to Dumpies – Destitute Unprepared Mature People.

April 1999

6

Business History

Let's Support the Inventors of Real Wealth

Who has added greatest value to British commerce since 1945? Sir Ernest Harrison of Racal? Lord Weinstock of GEC? Certainly those two generated enormous shareholder wealth and made themselves fortunes in the process. But there are other, almost unsung heroes who may not be so rich, but who have done wonders for industry and Britain. I am talking about the great inventors, a classic British breed.

I would argue that Sir James Black, the Scottish Nobel prize winner, has created more wealth than any of the above giants of business. Which company did he run? Well, he was neither chief executive nor chairman of any British firm. In fact he was the research scientist who discovered beta-blocker propranolol and anti-ulcer drugs – two of the most therapeutically and commercially successful drugs in history.

Black worked for ICI, SmithKline and Wellcome. His inventions helped build the UK pharmaceutical industry into one of our few post-war successes. Of course, he led a team of scientists who worked together to synthesize the drugs – in such fields no individual works alone. But he was undoubtedly the leader and the inspiration. Black has combined academic success with commercial achievement – a rare trick. There should be more like him.

Another pioneer who has achieved extraordinary things for mankind is Tim Berners-Lee. He is the genius who designed the world wide web, the crucial component that has made the internet such a powerful force for change. Never has such a new technology made such a rapid impact on so many aspects of life. The sudden wealth creation derived from the web is unprecedented. Yet Berners-Lee has never profited personally from it, even though he fully supports the involvement of business and applauds those who have become wealthy from it.

Again, he came from a university research background, and saw the point of the internet. He realised that by using computer hypertext systems and hardware networks, it would be possible to link computers globally to efficiently exchange packets of information. The web enables computers easily to share documents, databases, graphics, sound and video at no cost, so as to advance understanding. Perhaps no one this century has done more to improve global communication.

Ever since the web was devised, Berners-Lee has fought to ensure that the various software and hardware makers, service providers, and data suppliers and users keep it connecting people everywhere for free. His altruism and independence are remarkable. He remains the director of the World Wide Web Consortium, the co-ordinating body for web development, to keep it advancing. His story is told in his new autobiography, *Weaving the Web*.

These two great men are proof that we can still hack it when it comes to inventions and applying them. Throughout history, Britain has bred and trained great minds that have enriched the world immeasurably. Despite the complaints, our educational establishments can produce remarkable talent that delivers, and although many academics are theoreticians thank God some are not. In truth, the tough part about inventing is not the idea – the real challenge is putting it into action. Ultimately, we can all think of amazing things to invent – but most of us do nothing about it. The inventor doesn't just dream – he makes ideas happen.

The best recent books about British inventing were both written by successful home-grown inventors: James Dyson, who invented the Dual Cyclone vacuum cleaner, whose autobiography is *Against the Odds,* and Trevor Baylis, the inventor of the clockwork radio, whose autobiography *Clock This* has just been published.

Each book shows how the single most important trait an inventor must possess – apart from creative genius – is persistence. Without extraordinary determination, none of the four great men discussed above would have achieved so much to help make us richer. We owe our inventors a lot and one way to help would be to lobby Government to support the formation of an Academy of Invention, an idea put forward by Baylis. It would encourage and advise inventors and promote the idea of inventions in education and society as a whole. After all, 56 per cent of Japanese exports since 1945 have been based on British innovations. We should keep more of the rewards of our inventions. Our history shows we have the talent – we simply need to respect and harness it.

December 1999

Four of the Really Big Losers

The talk in business circles is of recession and slump. All around is worry and fear and failure. But such reverses are the very stuff of commercial life. As Voltaire said: "The progress of rivers to the ocean is not so rapid as that of man to error."

We all make mistakes, and we all try to learn from them. What is reassuring is that there have been plenty of business errors bigger than any you might ever make. By way of a reminder, I have compiled a list of a few messes over the years.

Nelson and Bunker Hunt are two sons of the fabled Texas oilman H.L. Hunt, once reputed to be the richest man alive. In 1979 and 1980 they tried to corner the silver market, and blew it. With Arab partners, the brothers accumulated 90m oz. of silver bullion and a similar amount of silver futures. The price climbed from about $10 per oz. to more than $50 per oz. on January 17th, 1980. On paper, the Hunts had made a profit of more than $3.5bn.

But they had reckoned without the little people deciding silver was overvalued. All over the world, old ladies were selling their silver tea sets and collectors their silver coins. In addition, the authorities limited further speculation in silver futures, destroying their corner. The price gradually declined until on March 27th, it collapsed from $15.80 to $10.80. The Hunts were left with debts of over $1.5bn, and various commodity firms they owed money to almost went bust. The brothers were forced to surrender many of their assets, and indeed by 1990 had been declared bankrupt.

When their elder sister asked Bunker what he had been playing at, the ex-billionaire replied: "Just trying to make some money."

Snapple became America's fastest-growing soft drink in the early 1990s, when it was controlled by a wily buyout-meister. It was caffeine-free and seen as healthy and "alternative". It was the king of New Age iced teas, carrying the slogan: "Made out of the Best Stuff on Earth." But it was a bubble.

Quaker Oats had been formed in 1901 and was the market

leader in oatmeals and cereals, and had enjoyed huge success with Gatorade thirst quencher, which has over 80 per cent of the US sports drink market. William Smithberg, Quaker's chairman and CEO, thought Snapple would compliment Gatorade beautifully. In 1994, he bought it for $1.4bn in cash. The price earnings exit multiple was in the stratosphere, but Quaker felt its marketing and distribution muscle could boost sales and cut Snapple's costs.

In fact it bought at the top. The success of Snapple spawned many copycats, while soft drink giants Coca-Cola and PepsiCo fought back hard against the upstart. Within 18 months Snapple was losing money. By 1997 Quaker had exhausted itself and sold the business for just $300m. It had lost over $2m a day on its investment.

Pearson made a prize foul-up in 1994 when it paid £312m for The Software Toolworks, which provided entertainment and education software to companies such as Sega and Nintendo. It bought the business on an exit p/e ratio of about 60. Lord Blakenham, the then chairman, described the deal as a "marvellous opportunity". In reality Pearson bought a business it didn't understand just as the CD-Rom market was about to collapse. It also suffered from the collapse in the video game cartridge market. Amazingly, Pearson said it had looked at over 120 prospective takeover candidates in the US before alighting on The Software Toolworks. It paid a stiff premium – at almost $15 a share, over seven times what the shares had changed hands for in mid-1993.

The business went wrong from the beginning. It started losing money within months of being acquired, and almost £50m before Pearson got rid of it earlier this year. The business changed its name to Mindscape, and Pearson added further acquisitions, taking its total cost to over $500m. It was sold for about £90m, giving Pearson a total write-off in excess of £250m within four years. This terrible deal contributed to the departure from Pearson of both Frank Barlow, the chief executive, and Blakenham.

The British arm of Hoover committed commercial suicide in

1992 by offering free air tickets to the United States to customers who bought a new appliance. The promotion turned into a catastrophe when more than 500,000 customers took up the opportunity of a free flight. The promotion ended in chaos and a flood of complaints from the public, who protested that they had not received tickets or flights they wanted.

Hoover soon faced a mass of litigation. By 1995 it had shelled out almost £50m in settlements, but it still faced over 375,000 claims. William Foust, president of Hoover Europe, was dismissed for his role in the misjudged promotion, which damaged Hoover's reputation as well as costing it tens of millions of pounds. Maytag, the US owner of Hoover Europe, lost patience with the whole debacle and eventually sold the business to Candy of Italy for £106m, a fraction of its worth a few years before.

November 1998

Coke, Big Mac and Harry Hyams

I recently wrote about some really bad large deals. It therefore only seems right that I should devote an article to a smattering of true excellent buys. The three I have chosen show that it can be worthwhile paying up for great assets.

The acquisition of Coca-Cola by Ernest Woodruff was one of the first recorded leveraged buyouts. The highly successful Southern soft drinks company was previously owned by the Chandler family. Asa Chandler, who had really developed the corporation, turned over his shares to his children in December 1917, and in August 1919 they sold to Woodruff's syndicate. Asa was horrified, and believed his accomplishments amounted to "ashes, just ashes".

The Chandlers received $15m in cash and $10m in 7 per cent preferred stock, a very large sum in those days. 500, 000 shares in a new corporation were issued and sold for $40 each on the first day's trading. The insiders within the syndicate received various lots of shares for $5 per share – Woodruff got 20,000 free. He and the other bankers – all part of the Trust Company of Georgia – controlled the voting within the new Delaware-registered Coca-Cola Corporation.

Effectively Woodruff paid no cash himself to gain control of the biggest business in Georgia. Coca-Cola became the largest beverage company in the world and possibly the best known consumer brand in history. One share of the original 1919 stock had split into 1,152 shares by 1991, in addition to providing a cumulative dividend of over $10,000. If the dividends from the original stock had been reinvested the $5 each share cost would now be worth more than $3m.

The purchase by Ray Kroc of McDonald's Restaurants was one of the great bargains, although it didn't seem it at the time. The business was established by Dick and Mac McDonald in Pasadena, California, in 1937. Kroc was a hard-driving milk-shake equipment salesman who saw the potential in the hamburger company, and became the master franchisee in April 1955 in Des Plains, near Chicago. He rapidly opened franchise outlets and by 1959 there were 100. He grew the business by owning the sites and having franchisees who paid a royalty as rent.

Eventually Kroc decided he needed to own the business, so in 1961 he paid the McDonald brothers $2.7m for the company – which he felt was a high price. He reasoned that it was he who had taken their formula and replicated it across America – but, nevertheless, he knew he had to buy them out to gain the freedom to grow the business. For that purchase price he got the brand, goodwill, and McDonald's Restaurants, which had combined sales of $37.8m.

Kroc managed to get a loan for the purchase price and within five years he had taken the business public on the New York Stock Exchange for more than 20 times what he paid for it in 1961. Kroc died in 1984, one of the richest men in the US. Today there are more than 22,000 McDonald's outlets across the world and the group is valued at over $47bn.

Possibly the most famous speculative office property development of the 1960s was London's Centre Point. This 34-storey skyscraper was finished in 1966 by Harry Hyams, through his property company, Oldham Estates. Hyams was one of the most secretive and successful of his generation of property men.

Centre Point was built where Tottenham Court Road intersects with Oxford Street. The London County Council wanted to change the road pattern but to do so it would have had to buy various freeholders, notably the Pearlberg family. This process was likely to take many years and LCC was unable to pay the ransom the Pearlbergs wanted. Hyams offered to provide the land for the new roads for nothing if the council gave him planning permission for Centre Point. He wanted a denser plot ratio for his office block than would normally have been allowed in return for solving the problem of the land for the new intersection.

Hyams bought out the Pearlbergs and the other freeholders and received consent for the 170,000 sq ft tower. All this took three years and the building cost perhaps £3.5m to erect. The LCC became the freeholder but granted a 150 year lease at £18,500 a year to Oldham Estates. Hyams probably paid a further £1.5m for the land, so the total investment was about £5m.

The theoretical rent on the building when completed would have been £1.16m, so assuming a 7 per cent yield, it would have had a value in 1966 of about £16.7m, or a profit of £11.7m, a return of more than 230 per cent.

Since then MEPC has bought Oldham Estates and Centre Point, but Hyams and the others maintain a minority share just to keep a check on the property giant. He also has more than 5 per cent of MEPC, worth in excess of £80m.

Inevitably, the building has appreciated in value over 30 years, although it would now be considered old fashioned – indeed, it is Grade 11 listed! The rent roll today if it were fully let would probably be £4m, which would give it a value of perhaps £70m.

November 1998

The First American Boss of the Tube

There have been some raised eyebrows at the arrival of Bob Kiley
from New York as Ken Livingstone's supremo for London's
transport system. How outrageous that an American should be in
charge of the London Underground! But in fact the true founder
and first boss of the London tube was an American, called Charles
Tyson Yerkes. Equally, there have been cries of distress at the
prospect of a privatised underground system. Yet the tube was
built as a venture for gain by private enterprise, effectively only
taken under state control in 1933.

So what of the first American tube supremo? Yerkes was born
in 1837 in Philadelphia of Welsh ancestry and Quaker parentage.
He became a clerk in a flour business and then a stockbroker in
1858. A few years later the ambitious young financier bought his
own investment bank. He was successful and well connected, and
started dealing in railway stocks and bonds, such as the
Seventeenth and Nineteenth Street Railway Company. He had
discovered his calling: financing railways.

But in 1871 the youthful stockbroker suffered a setback, when
the Great Chicago Fire triggered a nationwide financial panic, and
Yerkes' firm was plunged into bankruptcy. It was revealed that his
business had stolen money from the city of Philadelphia and lost
$400,000 of it, and Yerkes was jailed for 33 months. Yet the
irrepressible Yerkes was quoted while in prison:

"I have made up my mind to keep my mental strength
unimpaired, and think my chances for regaining my former
position, financially, are as good as they ever were."

The discredited financier received a pardon after serving seven
months of his sentence. Somehow by 1875 he had bought an
interest in the Continental Passenger Railway Company and saw
the stock climb from $15 to $100 a share. During this period he
also apparently posed as a colonel in Dakota. In 1881 he
decamped to Chicago, where he saw great opportunities in urban
transport.

By 1886 he and various associates had bought control of a North Side streetcar company, and his career as a mass-transit tycoon really took off. Within seven years he ran an empire that spanned the largest cable railway system in the United States with 290 miles of track and 7,000 staff. *Scientific American* magazine described him in 1893 in the following terms:

"Mr Yerkes now resides in Chicago, in the full enjoyment of his vast wealth and a sound mind and body, with a constantly increasing circle of business connections upon which to exercise his tremendous ability."

But not all the media were so kind. Then as now, the press attacked transport bosses relentlessly. Yerkes was hated more than most. He was reputed to have bribed the city council to obtain transport franchises, and used professional vamps to seduce and then blackmail politicians. They apparently openly sold Yerkes the use of the streets for cash. He also issued large flotations of watered stock, heaped securities upon securities and reorganisations upon reorganisations. He was bold in his promotions, stating: "The secret of success in my business is to buy old junk, fix it up a little and unload it upon other fellows."

His name will be known forever in Chicago not because he owned rail lines, but because he funded the building of the world's largest telescope in an attempt to become respectable and break into society. After he donated over $500,000 to the Yerkes Observatory, the *Chicago Evening Journal* ran a headline saying:

'Street Car Boss Uses Telescope as a Key to the Temple Door'

But despite his philanthropic endeavours in the field of astronomy, he remained vilified and an outcast in The Windy City. He started building the Loop Elevated system but was criticised and obstructed, so he gave up and sold all his US transit interests to New Yorkers Ryan and Whitney, and moved to London in 1900. Subsequently his American adventures were portrayed in Theodore Dreiser's great novel of crooked business, *The Financier*.

The so-called robber baron arrived in late Victorian London to find a nascent underground railway system – powered by steam.

The first Metropolitan line had opened in 1863, but there was little coherence to the various routes. Several lines had obtained building permissions but lacked funding. The arriviste railway promoter saw some old junk to buy and fix up. Yerkes quickly recruited Edgar Speyer, an American-born son of a German-Jewish banker, as a principal backer, together with the Old Colony Trust of Boston and moved into action.

In a flurry of acquisitions, Yerkes' American consortium took control of the District line in 1901, and later the Charing Cross, Euston & Hampstead Railway interests, the Brompton & Piccadilly Circus and the Great Northern & Strand – and then the Baker Street & Waterloo. By 1902, the conglomerate had been renamed the Underground Electric Railways Company of London Ltd and Yerkes was appointed its Chairman. This organisation became the basis for the Northern, District, Bakerloo, and Piccadilly lines. It is reputed that Yerkes decided to extend the Northern line beyond Hampstead, and open a depot at Golders Green, on a snap decision, based on a casual trip with his coachman.

For 60 years, no other tube lines were constructed. There are theories that Yerkes employed similar tactics of corruption to those he had adopted in Chicago in order to acquire his London underground network and keep out competition. The truth has never emerged, but Yerkes was quoted as stating: "It's the straphanger who pays the dividends."

The new system did not open for business as a whole until 1907, but Yerkes died in 1905 and never saw it in full flow. Nevertheless in five years he had welded together a chaotic group of half-completed lines, started the process of electrification and found the money to get them built. He may have been a convicted embezzler and an American, but he knew how to get the tube working. Let all of us who continue to use his creation hope that he set a precedent for efficiency and vigour which Mr Kiley can replicate.

February 2003

Georges Doriot

President George W. Bush is reputed to have said, "They don't even have a word for entrepreneur in France." Not only is the statement inaccurate, it is unfair to the many great French commercial innovators. Among them was a remarkable man called Georges Doriot, who became the father of modern venture capitalism.

Doriot was born in Paris in 1899 and served as an artillery officer in WWI. He left France in 1921 to attend the Harvard Business School (HBS). He was successful there and in 1926 became Professor in Industrial Management, and a legendary teacher. The expatriate Doriot took US citizenship and served as a Brigadier General during WWII under the US Quartermaster General. In the army he pioneered industrial and technology research: there is even a bulletproof vest called 'Doron' named after him.

His true calling came after he returned to HBS in June 1946, when he organised the world's first venture capital fund, called American Research & Development (ARD). It was a closed-end vehicle funded by local insurance companies and universities, and backed by Ralph Flanders of the Reserve Bank of Boston. The aim was to back early stage projects with risk equity over the longer term, and focus on technology coming out of Boston's various academic establishments – especially MIT. The managers of ARD were to give plenty of help to their fledgling investments. The first round of shares was sold at $25 each and $3.5 million was raised. The directors owned 45% of ARD, with the institutions the balance. Despite having a portfolio that included ten profitable companies, by 1951 the shares had sunk to $19. But Doriot and his small team persisted, charging just $9,000 a year to cover staff salaries.

The breakthrough came in 1957. Despite the recession of that year, ARD bought 77% of a new company called Digital Equipment Corporation (DEC) for $70,000. It was founded by

Ken Olsen and Harlan Anderson, engineers working in the Lincoln Laboratory at MIT. They wanted to compete with IBM in making computers, although initially they just made printed circuits. It was to prove one of the most spectacular investments of all time, and essentially inspired the formation of the entire venture capital industry.

After DEC made a profit in its first year, Doriot remarked: "I'm sorry to see this – no one has ever succeeded this soon and survived." But the Brigadier General proved a remarkable judge of character, and in Olsen he had backed one of the great entrepreneurs of the twentieth century. He believed that one should invest in "An A-quality man with a B-quality project, but not the other way round." With DEC he had A quality all-round. In 1959 DEC manufactured the first computer using a transistor, and subsequently invented the 'minicomputer' category of machine. Olsen was also an early exponent of Matrix management within DEC, with Doriot as his advisor and mentor. Within a few decades DEC grew to be the 27th largest corporation in the US with over 120,000 staff worldwide.

The growth of DEC and an earlier investment in High Voltage Engineering enabled Lehman to take ARD public in 1960 at an impressive $74.10 a share, raising $8 million. Doriot continued as President of the business until he was over 70, although he struggled to keep the best young venture capitalists working for him. They grew frustrated at their lack of ownership in ARD and the Brigadier General's refusal to share power. Several left to form other important VC firms, including Kleiner, Perkins, Caulfield & Buyers. Interestingly, no other such firms organised themselves as a public company: they were all private partnerships.

In 1972, ARD was sold to Textron Inc, the conglomerate, for an equivalent of $813 a share. It gave its original shareholders a compound annual return of over 15% for a period of almost 30 years, although fully half that profit came from its $355 million stake in DEC. It was a demonstration that in venture capital it is the big winners that count. DEC itself was eventually sold for almost $10 billion to Compaq in 1998, and is now part of HP. Doriot only died in 1987, and lived long enough to see the venture capital field expand to invest billions of dollars a year and revive US industry through the creation of such industrial giants as Microsoft and Federal Express. He was a versatile man: a teacher, a soldier, and a venture capitalist. He saw capital gains as 'a reward not a goal' and saw ARD as an experiment rather than purely a money making exercise. Such enlightened men are rare, and Brigadier General Georges Doriot deserves to be remembered.

October 2002

United Fruit

To find the first 20th century multinational you have to go to Central America. There, in the steamy jungle of Costa Rica, an entrepreneurial Brooklyn-born railroad man called Minor Keith established the United Fruit Company in 1899. He capitalised on the growing popularity of bananas, and created a business with a rich and highly political history – and helped make bananas the world's most widely consumed fruit.

United Fruit did not just grow and sell fruit: it effectively controlled whole economies. Over the decades, it grew to own over 1.7 million acres of land and over 1,000 miles of railroad in Guatemala, Honduras, Costa Rica, Panama, Columbia and Ecuador – while employing 60,000. Its power was such that it became known as the Octopus, and the nations where it operated as 'banana republics'.

From its founding, United Fruit was a monopolistic success – and riven with controversy. As one of its historians states: "Through bribery, fraud, chicanery, strong-arm tactics, extortion, tax evasion, and subversion it grew to be a swaggering behemoth." It regularly had anti-trust disputes with the US government, yet collaborated with the CIA to help maintain its dominance and remove the Communist threat from Latin America. Bloody strikes and disputes with socialist governments were regularly solved by the intervention of United States troops.

Despite its ruthless business practices, United Fruit was good at marketing bananas. It was helped by the 1923 success of Frank Silver's song "Yes, We Have No Bananas", and the cartoon character Miss Chiquita Banana, based on movie star Carmen Miranda. They pioneered the pitch that bananas were the perfect baby food and tasted delicious in breakfast cereal. By 1955 banana consumption had grown sixfold, and United Fruit was among the 100 largest US corporations.

In 1969, corporate raider Eli Black undertook the third largest transaction in Wall Street history to seize control of the company.

He merged it with his food conglomerate, AMK-John Morrell, and named the new entity United Brands. But the group had high debts and its plantations suffered from fungus attacks, hurricanes and new taxes. In 1974 the business lost $70 million, and on 3rd February 1975 Black committed suicide by jumping from the 44th window of the PanAm building in New York when the Securities and Exchange Commission discovered a $2.5 million bribe to a Honduran official.

By 1984 Carl Lindner, the richest man in Cincinnati, had bought a majority of the company and become President and Chairman. He sold non-core assets like its meatpacking interests and focused heavily on its historic core product – bananas. In 1989 the name was changed to Chiquita Brands International. By 1991 the group had recovered to make profits of $226 million on over $4.5 billion of sales. But the good times were not to last.

In recent years Chiquita Brands has suffered a series of setbacks. It over-invested in production capacity and custom-made reefer ships in the early nineties and racked up over $1 billion in debt. It anticipated an expanded European market but instead suffered from a new quota system that favoured ex-European colonies in the Caribbean. The Lindners have been generous donators to both US political parties and in return the US government imposed sanctions on the EU. Crop disease, rising costs and unhelpful weather all contributed to its problems. It has lost over $700 million in the last ten years and seen its stock price fall from over $50 to 72 cents. Meanwhile, its two major competitors, Dole and Del Monte, have coped with volatile markets rather better and taken market share. In November Chiquita suffered the ultimate indignity of going into Chapter 11, despite revenues of over $2 billion.

The company is likely to emerge from the bankruptcy process in a few months with improved prospects. Its lenders and bondholders will have undertaken a debt for equity swap and the current stockholders will end up with less than 10% of the restructured corporation. Meanwhile, last year the EU changed its banana quota system and the potential for Chiquita in the European market has revived. It might prove an interesting play for those with an appetite for high risk investments. No analysts now cover the company: control will transfer from the Lindner family and many of the new shareholders will be ex-bond holders who might dump the stock. No doubt its trading prospects will remain volatile, but it is still a powerful force in Central America and dominant in the banana business.

January 2002

A to Z

Many important books have been written about London, but the most useful must be the A-Z map. For over 65 years it has been the bible for anyone who needed to navigate the capital's confusing streets. Next to Harry Beck's diagrammatic tube map, it is the one thing any visitor to the capital needs to get around. More than sixty million copies have been sold – and the whole thing was the effort of a divorced thirty-year-old woman called Phyllis Pearsall.

This remarkable female entrepreneur had an unusual upbringing, as inventors so often do. She was the daughter of a Jewish Hungarian immigrant called Sandor Grosz and a mother who wrote radical plays and died in a lunatic asylum. Her father was a restless businessman who published maps for *The Daily Telegraph* under the name Geographia. He obviously inspired his daughter in her endeavours, with his resourceful, driven personality. But in 1920 he went bankrupt and moved to New York to start another business publishing guides.

Phyllis showed early artistic talent and married a painter in Paris. But she left him when they moved to Venice in 1935 and remained single and childless for the rest of her life. She returned to London and moved to a bedsitter in Horseferry Road. From there one evening she set off to a dinner party in Maida Vale. She was not a Londoner, and like many visitors, she got lost in the rain. She decided then that a handy map of London's streets was needed. So she set out to draw a plan of the city for herself.

The last charted map was the Ordnance Survey from 1919. Using this as a base, she spent a year walking the streets of London, recording every road using her skills as a draughtswoman. She worked 18-hour days with a superhuman sense of purpose, a slight, lonely figure sketching streets, their names and house numbers. She tramped 3,000 miles and covered 23,000 streets. Phyllis possessed a remarkable determination. She battled to get the book produced professionally, and sold her street atlas herself by cold-calling on shops. Her first break came with a big order from WHSmith, secured after receiving endless snubs because she was a woman 'rep'. She delivered the initial batches using a wheelbarrow.

Very quickly the A-Z became an indispensable book for anyone who wanted to know their way around London. Phyllis displayed vision and persistence of a rare kind, fighting against prejudice and complacency in the cartographic, publishing and retail trades. In time A-Z assumed a position as the dominant guide to the capital, and despite various imitators it remains the generic name, like Hoover or Sellotape. The founder of The Geographers' Map Company suffered a number of awful setbacks, including terrible injuries from a plane crash in 1946 and two strokes, but she survived and her business prospered.

She continued as Chairman of her creation until her death in 1996. The business grew to encompass maps for cities across Britain, atlases and road maps – in all over 250 titles. It remains proudly independent and successful, thanks to her generosity in establishing a special trust, modelled on The John Lewis Partnership structure. In effect the staff control the A-Z business and have ensured its continuing success. Phyllis encouraged the use of new technology and the business was an early adopter of computerised mapping techniques. These have helped keep A-Z pre-eminent, even though it is a small organisation compared to many rival publishers. It retains a motto she provided: "On We Go."

Mrs Phyllis Pearsall was an accomplished artist and grew to love London's fascinating history through her interest in its streets and buildings. She wrote an excellent autobiography, *From Bedsitter to Household Name: The Personal Story of A-Z Maps*, and a recent biography, *Mrs P's Journey*, by Sarah Hartley, has just been published. Both books are wonderful inspiration to anyone who has an exciting new idea and needs encouragement. The story of Phyllis Pearsall is a special motivator for women who want to do something bold and different. There are perhaps all too few stories of brilliant British women who build lasting enterprises against the odds: Phyllis was one of the pioneers.

December 2001

Airline Pioneers

The airline business has always attracted daredevils and showmen. From Howard Hughes to Kirk Kerkorian, many fortunes have been made and lost flying planes in an attempt to turn a profit. In truth, civil aviation has been a boom and bust game since the day it started, with the world's first daily international air service from Hounslow Heath to Paris on 25th August 1919, operated by Aircraft Transport and Travel Limited. Supposedly, the industry has generated a net trading loss since its founding, but despite these poor economics quite a few outstanding entrepreneurs have done well from it.

These days the independent kings of the sky across Britain are Sir Richard Branson of Virgin Atlantic, Sir Michael Bishop of British Midland, Stelios Haji-Iounnou of easyJet, and Michael O'Leary of Ryanair. The latter two are champions of the no-frills air travel revolution, which has transformed the way we take holidays.

They owe an element of their success to a pioneer of discount travel, Sir Freddie Laker. He served for five years as Managing Director of British United Airways and then started out on his own, creating Laker Airways in 1966, using second hand airliners from BOAC. Initially a short-haul charter service, Laker undercut the established rivals' fares by offering a more basic service. In September 1977 he launched Skytrain, the first low-cost scheduled transatlantic flights, from Gatwick to New York. Tickets cost £59 one-way, under half the lowest fare from the competition. He was an important early customer of Airbus, helping them to become the only real rival airliner manufacturer to Boeing.

Sadly, Laker Airways went bust in February 1982, owing over £300 million. A recession, unfavourable exchange rate movements, and high levels of debt saw the upstart service grounded. Later several major carriers paid compensation to Sir Freddie and the liquidator of his airline, settling accusations that they were operating a cartel in conjunction with the aircraft makers.

But perhaps the greatest airline entrepreneur of all time was Juan Terry Trippe, founder of Pan Am. More than any other man, he invented mass air travel. A Yale graduate from a well-to-do Baltimore family, he went into the aviation business at the age of 24, forming an air taxi service along the East Coast of the US by buying six ex-navy training seaplanes. Later he created a new airline to carry mail, called Aviation Company of the Americas. In 1928, this merged with a rival to form Pan Am. Its first flight carried US post from Key West to Havana.

Trippe understood perfectly that the airline business is part engineering, part finance, part politics – and part chutzpah. Throughout his long career, he bet the company on major advances in aeronautical technology, convinced of a long term rise in demand for air travel. Meanwhile he persuaded his rich pals from Yale, and later Wall Street, to back his hunches on passenger growth. All the while he assiduously cultivated contacts in Washington, ensuring Pan Am was always well treated by the legislators.

By the early 1930s Pan Am was the world's largest airline and the sole US international carrier, thanks to its network in Central and South America. Trippe recruited the legendary Charles Lindbergh to act as advisor and ambassador for the corporation. Gradually passenger air traffic took off, with Pan Am being the first to encourage tourist class customers – not just the very rich.

In 1958 Pan Am instituted one of the first non-stop transatlantic services – using jet planes. Later the airline backed Boeing's 707 aircraft – and then placed a $550 million order for the first 747 Jumbo jets – the largest commercial transaction in history in 1966. Trippe unexpectedly announced his retirement at the Pan Am AGM in 1968, before the Jumbo had been introduced. The company gradually fell apart following his departure: deregulation increased competition, and the Lockerbie terrorist outrage on Pan Am Flight 103 in December 1988 finally killed the business.

Trippe died in 1981 but his legacy lives on. Since 9/11 aviation has suffered increased security costs, sharply fluctuating demand, and a steep hike in fuel costs. But despite the US airline industry being battered with bankruptcies, successful start-ups like JetBlue, run by David Neeleman, have shown it's still possible to make good margins in the carrier business if you do it right. His business is low-fare but with in-flight extras like movies, and has non-unionized staff. It has no airport hub but flies point to point, and uses just two types of plane. JetBlue is only six years old, but enjoying healthy profits. The industry remains as treacherous as any, but is still open to brave individuals who fancy their chances.

January 2006

Alfred Nobel

Alfred Nobel was perhaps the most famous Swede who ever lived. He combined the life of an inventor with that of an industrialist on a hugely successful scale over several decades of the 19th century. But it was only in 1895, the year before his death, that he made the decision to leave the majority of his estate to the creation of the Nobel Prizes – and it for this that he will be remembered by billions of people across the world.

He was born in 1833 in Stockholm; his father, Immanuel Nobel, was an inventor who pioneered modern plywood. After the bankruptcy of the family firm, they moved to St Petersburg to manufacture munitions. There Alfred and his three brothers received private tuition in science and the arts; by the age of 17 he could speak and write Swedish, French, Russian, English and German. This helped foster his cosmopolitan outlook on life. Later he studied chemistry in France and then returned to Sweden to experiment with nitroglycerine, an explosive compound discovered by Ascanio Sobrero, a fellow student, in 1847.

Alfred incorporated nitroglycerine into an absorbent, inert earthy sand and formed the material into sticks, which made it safer to handle. He named his invention dynamite after the Greek word for power, *dynamis*, and received a patent for it in 1863 when he was just 30. A year later a terrible explosion wrecked the family factory and killed his brother Emil and several staff, but Alfred persisted, and that same year he incorporated a joint stock company with a local merchant banker to exploit his new product.

His timing was fortunate. All over Europe and America there were huge infrastructure projects underway, such as tunnelling and bridge building – many of which required rock blasting. Nobel's new explosive, especially combined with his other invention – the detonator or blasting cap – made the process dramatically easier. Moreover, the mining industry was expanding with the introduction of the diamond bit and the pneumatic drill; dynamite helped still further. Alfred went to Germany, France,

America, Britain and Italy, finding partners to fund local dynamite factories. Nobel contributed his patent and kept anywhere up to 50% of each enterprise. Ultimately they merged to form the Nobel Dynamite Trust Company, one of the world's first multinational holding companies. Even though Nobel said that he "cordially hated commerce", he was clearly a genius at it, having pioneered a highly sophisticated form of financing for large scale chemical manufacture.

Nobel kept a home in Paris rather than Sweden, but spent his time shuttling between laboratories in various countries carrying out experiments. Victor Hugo nicknamed him "Europe's richest vagabond." By the time of his death he had 355 patents to his name and claimed the invention of smokeless gunpowder, or cordite, among other things. Late in his career he bought Bofors, the giant Swedish arms maker, and had huge success helping his two brothers in their massively profitable oil business Branobel in Baku, now the capital of Azerbaijan.

A turning point in his life came in 1888, when his brother died, and a Parisian newspaper confused the two Nobel brothers. In the misguided obituary they wrote: "Le marchand de la mort est mort" and "Dr Alfred Nobel, who became rich by finding more ways to kill more people faster than ever before, died yesterday." Alfred decided he would ensure his legacy was more than that of a merchant of death. He therefore signed a will leaving the majority of his estate to award "prizes to those who, during the preceding year, shall have conferred the greatest benefit to mankind."

He chose to honour the disciplines of physics, chemistry, and medicine, and create prizes for great works of literature and advances in peace. His gift had a profound effect on the history of modern science and the arts in the 20th century. He never married and had no direct descendants, but through his inventions and foundation he achieved a degree of immortality granted to very few. Far more than just a plutocratic Swedish chemist, Nobel also wrote poetry and drama, and even has a synthetic element named after him: Nobelium. For the past 105 years, the world's academics have valued his prizes beyond any other accolades. He wrote: "I am sick of the explosives trade, wherein one continually stumbles over accidents, restrictive regulations, red tape, pedants, knavery, and other nuisances." Yet dynamite made Nobel rich and so gave the world a lasting monument to intellectual endeavour, perhaps as reparations for its destructive powers.

April 2006

Who Remembers the Founder of GM?

It is wrong to think that business is all about money and hard facts. The truth is that it is riddled with emotion and subject to whims of ego and fashion.

But what does seem absent in business is nostalgia and sentimentality. The "creative destruction" of capitalism has no time to be misty-eyed about the past. Entrepreneurs never look backwards – only to the future.

And so great titans of business are soon forgotten, as are the huge firms they create when they are sold and wither. Names and products disappear once they are superseded.

Occasionally the reputation of a great figure of commerce might last – characters such as JP Morgan or John D. Rockefeller have both had biographies written about them. Others such as Walt Disney live on through their creations. But mostly the rich and powerful, who once ruled kingdoms of trade, are less well remembered than minor poets, actors, singers, writers, painters, comedians and even politicians. We have no memory for magnates.

A classic example of such a forgotten hero of business is William Crapo Durant, the founder of General Motors. Not only does GM have more sales than any other business in the world, it is also the largest player in the largest manufacturing industry on earth. And one man essentially built the firm. But ask a GM employee or customer who he was or look for a history of the man and you will find nothing.

If he had been dull or uninspiring, then that might be understandable: but in fact Durant was an extraordinary man during an amazing era.

Durant started making horse-drawn carriages on his own account when only 24 in 1886 in Flint, Michigan. From the beginning his vision and sales grew the company rapidly, both organically and by purchasing companies to supply parts for his wagons and buggies. He found able staff, organised, motivated, and persuaded competitors to sell out and was forever thinking bigger.

Soon his business was the largest carriage maker in the US. By the time he was 40, in 1902, he had become rich and outgrown the Durant-Dort Carriage Company: he moved from Michigan to New York City to seek pastures new.

These he found in 1904 in the fledgling automobile industry, which over 15 years led to the disappearance of the carriage-making trade. He salvaged the Buick Motor Company, which soon became the largest automaker around.

From 1908 he began a process of consolidation of vehicle and component makers in a whirlwind of mergers. Within two years he had brought 25 companies, including Cadillac and Olds into General Motors Corporation. He vertically integrated the business by buying parts makers in order to achieve economies of scale and efficiencies of production. Despite the speed of its assembly, GM was successful and profitable from its inception.

In 1910 Durant lost control of the business to a banking syndicate during a sudden recession, but he promptly proceeded to form the Chevrolet Motor Company, which was also a winner.

By 1915 he had regained control of GM, and once more expansionist policies were to the fore. GM also became Canada's largest auto maker and the biggest truck builder, and a market leader in fridges as well as vehicle finance.

Unfortunately, Durant over-extended himself in the stock market and was finally kicked out of GM for good by the du Ponts in 1920. He then proceeded to create a new automobile business called the Durant Motor Company when he was 60. But Durant couldn't administer and it failed some years later.

Despite this reverse, he was hugely active in Wall Street until the crash in 1929, and was known as "King of the Bulls". But again he borrowed too much on margin, and eventually in 1936 he was declared bankrupt. He died in near poverty and virtual obscurity in 1946.

As much as Henry Ford, Durant invented the modern motor industry. General Motors pioneered vertically-integrated car manufacturing and the concept of a whole range of vehicles for different types of customer. During Durant's heyday, the US grew to be the greatest economic power on earth, powered by the auto trade.

W.C. Durant built the auto business, which in turn built America. But capitalists like him do not enjoy the immortality granted to great men of war or the arts. Their achievements are seen as transient and a by-product of their money grabbing. Most companies die just as their founders do. They lack the romance of those whose successes are more intangible but perhaps more moving. Even when they die vastly rich and titled, within a generation they are all but forgotten, overtaken by hungry newcomers building their own commercial empires.

August 2000

The Panama Canal

I have always greatly admired huge infrastructure projects, even if they mostly turn out to be rotten investments – at least for the founding subscribers. Perhaps the outstanding modern day example of this genre is Eurotunnel, the 50km undersea link between Britain and France. After a cost of £12 billion – almost three times the original estimate – and huge write-offs by shareholders, lenders and contractors, the project opened in 1994 and is now used by 20 million travellers a year. It was entirely privately financed, and is perhaps the finest engineering achievement of the 20th century. But its history is relatively uncomplicated compared to the extraordinary tale of the Panama Canal.

The real initiator of a shipping link across the Panamanian isthmus between the Pacific and Atlantic Oceans was a French promoter called Vicomte Ferdinand de Lessops. Previously he had been behind the successful construction of the Suez Canal, connecting the Mediterranean to The Indian Ocean, and was perhaps the most famous citizen in France. He determined to tackle another bold scheme, and in 1879 he chartered the Compagnie Universelle du Canal Interoceanique to build 'La Grande Tranchee' for a projected $240 million in Panama, then part of Columbia. Creating the Panama Canal would save ships a 12,000 mile trip around the tip of South America. At the time it was the greatest human undertaking ever attempted.

But la grande enterprise was flawed from the start, with poor designs and planning. Despite 20,000 labourers excavating the strait, progress was slow owing to incompetent logistics, landslides and workers getting infected with yellow fever, tuberculosis and malaria. By 1889 the money had run out with only a fifth of the canal completed, and the Compagnie Universelle was bankrupt, having lost $290 million. The failure saw thousands of peasants across Europe lose their life savings, and the organisers such as de Lessops – and even Gustave Eiffel – were imprisoned for fraud.

In 1894 the business was recapitalized as The Compagnie Nouvelle, with a view to reviving the canal and recouping some of the vast losses. An enigmatic French adventurer called Philippe Bunau-Varilla, who had been head of excavation in the Compagnie Universelle, recruited William Nelson Cromwell, a powerful New York lawyer, to convince the US government to buy the French assets in Panama and build the canal for strategic and commercial reasons. By 1900 these assets consisted principally of a concession from Columbia to build the canal and the Panama Railroad Company – itself originally organised by New York financiers.

Despite the passing by Congress in January 1902 of a bill approving the construction of a canal through Nicaragua instead, Cromwell convinced President Teddy Roosevelt to support the Panama passage. So in August that year the Senate reversed the House vote and adopted the Panama route, with approval to buy up the French assets for $40 million. However, Columbia felt it should receive a large portion of any such largesse, and in 1903 it rejected the proposed Panama Canal treaty. Cromwell saw that his French clients might lose out, and he helped instigate a revolution in Panama. Roosevelt, the youngest man ever to be president and an unashamed imperialist, became convinced that only an independent Panama would permit the US to safeguard its maritime interests. So the revolution duly took place in November, with the loss of one human life and one donkey.

Meanwhile the double-dealing Cromwell had secretly assembled a syndicate of wealthy backers, including financier JP Morgan and Republican presidential candidate William Taft, to buy up as much stock and bonds of the bankrupt French Panama company as possible for around 3% of face value. They spent about $3.5 million, and then turned their stake to the US government for over $24 million. A scandalous expose in Pulitzer's 'World' newspaper published details in 1904 of the conspiracy to wrest Panama away from Columbia and make a stock market killing. Four years later Roosevelt filed a libel suit, but his case was dismissed.

The canal itself took another ten years to build, using a series of locks, and opened for shipping in 1914. It eventually cost $639 million, but dramatically speeded shipping times as intended. In a speech in 1911, Roosevelt admitted "...I took the Isthmus," and consequently the US Congress paid Columbia $25 million reparations in 1922 for taking Panama. In 1979 President Jimmy Carter signed a new treaty that dissolved the Canal Zone, and also guaranteed Panama's neutrality. Using that pretext, the US invaded Panama in 1989 to capture General Noriega, the brutal despot, who was eventually sentenced to forty years in prison for drug smuggling. Today the Panama Canal is no longer the vital waterway it once was, and was duly transferred back under the control of The Republic of Panama on 31st December 1999.

August 2001

Selfridges and Whiteley's

It seems traditional department stores are a dying breed: the Allders chain shut last year, and both Barkers and Dickens & Jones are to cease trading. But a century ago, it was a very different affair: then, the giant shopping emporia were all the rage, and the department store magnates were real high rollers who led extraordinary lives.

Among the great retailing pioneers, few can match the achievements of William Whiteley, the so-called 'Universal Provider' of Victorian London. He travelled to London from his home in Yorkshire in 1855, aged just 24, to learn the drapery trade. After six years' apprenticeship and having saved £700, he opened a small shop in an unfashionable district called Bayswater.

Over the next twenty years his business grew steadily, and he gradually bought more property in and around Westbourne Grove and what is now Queensway, eventually controlling an empire covering 14 acres. He sold a huge range of goods: his slogan was 'Everything from a pin to an elephant'. He undercut local traders and was a ruthless competitor – perhaps as a consequence his shop was subject to five serious arson attacks.

In the late 19th century Whiteley's became the leading department store in London, and the company went public on the London Stock Exchange in 1899. Over 6,000 staff were employed in the business, most of them living in company accommodation, and working from 7am to 11pm, six days a week. Whiteley bought farmlands and built food-processing factories to provide produce for the store, and in 1896 earned an unsolicited royal warrant from Queen Victoria.

But despite the huge success of his business and Whiteley's public reputation as a great benefactor, in private he was a bully and philanderer. He was a tyrant towards his workers and seduced shop girls with impunity. Eventually his wife grew tired of his infidelity, and sued for divorce on the grounds of adultery and cruelty. On 24th January 1907, his disreputable behaviour caught up with him. A man called Horace Rayner, who claimed to be Whiteley's illegitimate son, shot Whiteley twice in the head, killing him instantly, and then attempted suicide.

At his trial for murder, Rayner claimed temporary insanity, but was nevertheless found guilty and sentenced to death. However, when the truth about Whiteley came out, public sympathy forced the Home Secretary to commute the sentence to life imprisonment. Whiteley's two sons attempted to continue the operation and opened a magnificent new shop in 1912, but in due course the business was sold to Whiteley's arch rival, Gordon Selfridge.

Selfridge was born in Wisconsin in 1858, the same state as Henry Wellcome, who also came to Britain to make a great fortune. At the age of 21 he went to Chicago and joined what was to become Marshall Field & Co. Over 25 years he rose to become a junior partner and amassed a considerable fortune. In 1906 he travelled to London with his wife Rosalie and decided to open a US-style department store at the unfashionable Western end of Oxford Street. He aimed "to make my shop a civic centre, where friends can meet and buying is only a secondary consideration." He spent £400,000 on the project: Selfridges opened in 1909 and was an immediate hit.

The business grew rapidly and went public. Selfridges set new standards for the retail trade, and its founder was credited with the phrase 'The customer is always right'. Selfridge enjoyed a true tycoon's lifestyle and lived in splendid Lansdowne House off Berkeley Square in London (now the Lansdowne Club) and Highcliffe Castle in Hampshire.

But his personal spending outstripped his resources, and when the business suffered during the Great Depression, he found himself financially overextended. In 1931 he was nearly bankrupted when the Inland Revenue claimed £150,000 in tax, and finally in 1940 the Directors of Selfridges voted to remove him from the Board as Chairman and give him the honorary title of President on just £2,000 a year. He died almost forgotten in Putney in 1947 aged 90, with just £1,500 to his name.

Today Whiteley's is a shopping mall owned by Standard Life, while Selfridges remains London's best department store with over 500,000 square feet of shopping space. It was taken over in 2003 and is now owned by Galen Weston. In commerce, there is little room for sentiment – yet sometimes the stories are worth recording. Sadly today, there is little record visible to the public in either establishment of the epic rise and tragic fall of the two extraordinary characters who created the original stores. Remember them next time you go shopping.

October 2005

Richard Cobden

For the past ten years I have been Chairman and part-owner of The Cobden Club, a fine Victorian edifice in North Kensington. These days it is a venue for refreshment and entertainment of every variety: but it also has a fascinating history of a different kind.

It was established in 1866 to promote the views of Richard Cobden, the so-called 'Apostle of Free Trade'. Cobden had died the year before. On his death, Disraeli proclaimed him "an ornament to the House of Commons and an honour to England." He was probably the most influential 19th century British politician never to have held office under the Crown. What is truly extraordinary is that Cobden remains 140 years later a hero for proponents everywhere of globalisation, and believers in the ability of free markets to promote peace among trading nations.

Cobden was born in 1804 and trained in the textile trade. He started a partnership undertaking calico printing when he was 24, and settled in Manchester four years later. Although he was a successful entrepreneur, he also possessed a restless intellect, and in 1835 published a pamphlet advocating the abolition of trade tariffs between countries. This cause became his life's mission. Gradually he gave up business for politics. He became an alderman in Manchester, and in 1841 the MP for Stockport. He campaigned vigorously for the repeal of the notorious Corn Laws, which were in effect a tax on bread. Cobden believed their abolition would help maximise popular welfare and forge bonds of peace between nations. In 1846 Sir Robert Peel, the Prime Minister, relented and the Corn Laws were scrapped by the Commons. Cobden had achieved his first great objective.

But he could not retire from the political fray. "Why should I rust in inactivity?" Cobden demanded of himself. He continued to crusade on an anti-protectionist platform, and his final triumph came in 1860 with a pioneering treaty of commerce with the French which he spearheaded. He was offered a baronetcy and a seat on the Privy Council by Lord Palmerston, but refused and remained an independent to the end. A measure of his international standing was the official French announcement that his passing was "a cause for mourning for France and humanity." Partly thanks to Cobden, the 19th century saw an unprecedented freedom of movement for people, goods and capital – and perhaps the most sustained period of peace in modern history.

Cobden was a successful capitalist, and saw how the 'animal spirits' it releases can advance society as a whole. I believe there are three principal reasons for this:

- Capitalism is not a zero-sum game: those who do business together generate new wealth and jobs and add value – they do not tend simply to recycle existing work and money;

- Capitalism gives ordinary people hope – they too can become prosperous, with hard work and a little luck; and

- Capitalism breeds peace, because nations that trade have too much to lose by fighting.

For the proof of the last assertion, it is worth referring to the Human Security Report, a definitive study of worldwide conflicts published last year by the OUP. It documents the dramatic but largely unknown decline in the numbers of wars, genocides and human rights abuses over the last decade or so. This coincides with the upswing in enterprise across many ex-communist states in Eastern Europe, Asia, and the rise of China and India as de facto capitalist economies. Economic freedom tends to drive democracy and reduce the corruption that festers in totalitarian states, where private property is anathema. Cobden realised that liberalisation of trade is a moral imperative: it helps reduce poverty and inequality, increases life expectancy, and promotes education.

As a statesman it would be hard to find Cobden's equivalent today. He started as a manufacturer, but gave up a life of certain wealth for a career as a radical activist, outside the party system. He understood first hand the profundity of Samuel Johnson's remark: "There are few ways in which a man can be more innocently employed than getting money." He worked tirelessly for a moral belief, and rejected the bribes and baubles which infect most politicians. His profound insight into human affairs and motivation helped build create modern society. At a time when protectionism and barriers to trade are on the rise in countries like France, Spain and Poland, the world needs to remember the political philosophy of The Apostle of Free Trade. I'm proud that The Cobden Club bears his name.

March 2006

George Hudson

Entrepreneurs are often hated and admired in equal measure, and none more so than the consummate 19th century 'projector' George Hudson. A resilient Yorkshireman, he became "a railway autocrat, with greater power than the Prime Minister" in the space of fifteen years. But his huge success was short-lived, and he was ultimately disgraced and exiled when his empire crashed. A wonderful new biography, *The Railway King*, by Robert Beaumont, provides a balanced and highly readable view of his achievements and shortcomings, and offers great insight into the psychology of the business-builder, a person for whom "The great end of life is not knowledge, but action."

Hudson was born the son of a farmer in 1800, and ran away from home to York after he fathered an illegitimate child at the age of 15. He became an apprentice draper and managed to marry the boss's daughter and become a partner in the shop at 24. The defining moment in his life came a few years later when he was left £30,000 by a Great Uncle who had changed his will at the last moment. This considerable fortune enabled him to pursue ambitious schemes, the first of which was the York Union Bank, an entity Hudson co-founded in 1833.

In 1825 the steam railway era had commenced with the founding of the Stockton and Darlington line, and Hudson enthusiastically became Treasurer of the York Railway Committee to promote a rail connection to the cathedral city. He joined the local Tory party and was appointed Chairman of the York and North Midland Railway in 1836. The following year the unscrupulous and confident Hudson was elected Lord Mayor of York. By 1839 the railroad had opened and The Railway King was on his way.

During the 1840s a railway mania erupted in Britain, reminiscent of the internet frenzy of recent times. Hundreds of new lines were promoted and tens of millions invested by the undiscerning public. Hudson created the Midland Railway through a merger of two struggling lines in 1843 and became its Chairman. He partnered with the genius railway engineer George Stephenson. By the spring of 1846 he controlled four major rail networks including the York, Newcastle and Berwick and the Eastern Counties. At his zenith, he chaired companies that owned 1,500 miles out of the total track of 5,000 miles. Over 200,000 labourers worked on constructing his lines. Hudson owned Albert Gate East, the largest private residence in London, and served as MP for Sunderland. He had rapidly become one of the richest and most famous men in Britain.

Unfortunately, he conducted business in a haphazard manner, and his personal and corporate dealings were confused. While his companies paid dividends there were no complaints: but the orgy of speculation, the repeal of The Corn Laws and rising interest rates led to an economic depression in 1847. A highly critical pamphlet called 'The Bubble of The Age' was published, attacking Hudson. Rail traffic dwindled, dividends were cut, and The Railway King's many enemies gathered for the kill. He was accused of insider dealing, bribery, paying dividends out of capital, and selling assets to his companies at a profit. Critics like the historian Macaulay called him "a bloated, vulgar, insolent, purse-proud, greedy, drunken blackguard."

While Hudson argued he had been "morally right, but legally wrong", his rivals pursued him for gross improprieties. His brother-in-law committed suicide over his involvement in the growing scandal in 1849 and Hudson absconded to France to escape bankruptcy. His snobbish and hypocritical opponents denounced his career as "one vast aggregate of avaricious and flagitious jobbing for the accumulation of wealth." In truth, they resented the uneducated but enthusiastic Northerner, for he "united largeness of view with wonderful speculative courage" and possessed "a faculty of amalgamation." But it was ever thus in our nation – resentment among the establishment and the intelligentsia for those of energy who make their own fortunes. Despite the seeming disgrace, Hudson was never convicted of any criminal offence and retained many admirers to the end.

In truth Hudson's legacy was a series of remarkable public works, ranging from the Sunderland Docks to the foundations of the country's modern railway network. His vaulting ambition, hot temper, and inadequate administration did for him, along with his excessive drinking. But then as now, corruption and incompetence in railway finance were as much a fault of the system as the entrepreneurs who built and ran the trains. From the 1840s to Railtrack, it seems our train networks are permanently bedevilled by chaos and insolvency. Hudson's whole career was a mad romance aimed at annihilating distance. He was an English founder, warts and all, of the Modern Age.

March 2002

Sir Henry Wellcome

Who has been the most successful British entrepreneur of all time? An impossible question to answer, of course; but a strong candidate would be Sir Henry Wellcome, founder of Wellcome plc – now part of Glaxo SmithKline – and the vastly influential Wellcome Trust. Yet Henry Wellcome was actually a naturalised Briton, and many of his characteristics – his salesmanship, his business acumen, his outstanding philanthropy – can in part be attributed to his American upbringing. Nevertheless, I put him forward as a contender.

Wellcome was born to a poor but devout family of farmers in Wisconsin in 1853. At the age of 15, inspired by an uncle who was a doctor, Wellcome left home to become a prescription clerk at a pharmaceutical chemist on the East Coast. He then studied pharmacy in Philadelphia and graduated in 1874. He promptly got a job as a travelling drug salesman for McKesson in New York, a powerful wholesale druggist.

After six years learning the trade he renewed his acquaintance with Silas Burroughs, who ran a successful drug supply company specialising in new products called compressed medicine tablets – or pills. They formed a business partnership with capital of £2,000, and Wellcome left for England – where tablets were entirely novel. He had no money to fund the enterprise, but contributed his exclusive licence for McKesson's products which his old employer had granted him. At the age of 26, Wellcome had become an entrepreneur.

The goods he sold initially were mostly cosmetic rather than curative in their effects. But the American druggist still taught the complacent local pharmaceutical industry how to market medicines. The company grew rapidly, and in 1883 opened a manufacturing plant in Wandsworth, South London. From here Burroughs Wellcome produced its pioneering 'tabloid' preparations that helped revolutionise the British drug market.

Unfortunately, both partners in the expanding firm had

considerable ambition and in 1887 they fell out. Their disputes dragged on for some years and were only settled on Burroughs' death in 1895. While Burroughs had been a formidable salesman, Wellcome was an administrator of genius, and saw the need for drug companies to invest in research and develop their own new medicines. He bought out his late partner's share in the business for just over £113,000 and became the sole owner.

Wellcome now put more emphasis on discovering new drugs and the business opened its own Physiological and Chemical Laboratories. He understood how to combine ethical scientific research with commercial aims – something the British still find difficult. And he at last spared time for a personal life, marrying Syrie – the daughter of the famous Dr Barnardo – in 1901. But it was not a happy union, and within ten years they had separated – she later married the novelist Somerset Maugham. The pharmaceutical company however grew from strength to strength, expanding into serum and vaccine products, and veterinary medicine. By 1910 Wellcome was a multi-millionaire, as the business opened successful branches in the British colonies, in addition to its core British and American operations.

Over the years Wellcome became an avid archaeologist and collector, and many of these artefacts and documents are now housed at the Science Museum and Wellcome Library in London. In 1902 he established a tropical diseases laboratory in Khartoum in Sudan, which had been annexed by the British. Public health in the country improved dramatically as a result.

In his later years Wellcome was a solitary and difficult figure. Although he had a son, Mounteney, he bequeathed his lifetime's achievements to his own charity. In 1936 Wellcome died and left a Trust and a pharmaceutical business – both to be active in medical research. Death Duties and WWII hindered progress, but from the 1950s the American arm of the business took off. Important drugs such as Septrin, Zyloric and Imuran were conceived and sales grew from £50 million in the late 1960s to £400 million by 1977. Later blockbuster products included

Retrovir and Zovirax. In 1986 Wellcome plc was taken public, and merged with Glaxo in 1995. The trust has gradually reduced its stake in the emergent company, such that it is now by far the largest benefactor to British medical research – even outspending the government. Its munificence is an extraordinary and lasting memorial to the brilliant, but troubled Victorian pharmacist from Wisconsin.

October 2003

7

Investing

The Key Questions About Every Investment

Before investing your money in a company, you should do your homework. Only when you have the answers to these 50 key questions will you be able to evaluate the investment risk and rewards.

1. What experience and track record do the chief executive, finance director and other senior executives have?

2. How stable is the management team and how are they regarded from within their industry, and by financial journalists, analysts and fund managers?

3. What is the background and quality of the non-executive directors?

4. What shareholding do the board own, and have they bought or sold shares in the recent past?

5. Who are the auditors and stockbrokers?

6. How long-established is the business and how good is its track record?

7. Who are its major competitors?

8. What are the barriers to entry and how great are they?

9. Are the company's products or services long-life or subject to rapid change?

10. What is the mix of the business across its various product and service categories?

11. Who are the company's principal customers, and what percentage of its business is derived from its three biggest customers?

12. How big is the overall market and what is its market share?

13. Is the industry growing and, if so, how fast?

14. Is the marketplace fragmented or is it fairly concentrated?

15. Who are the principal suppliers to the company and how dependent is it on them?

16. Does the company have unique competitive advantages, such as patents, brands, copyrights, designs or technology?

17. Is the company heavily regulated or unionised?

18. What are its greatest strengths and weaknesses?

19. What are the greatest opportunities and threats to the company?

20. Does the company undertake research and development and, if so, how much does it spend?

21. What is the company's annual capital expenditure and how does this compare to its depreciation charge?

22. Has the company grown organically or has it undertaken acquisitions to expand?

23. Are there other companies to buy or are there no obvious acquisitions left?

24. If there are other firms to buy, would they be available at a sensible price?

25. Is the company heavily borrowed and, if so, at what cost and who are its bankers?

26. What is its interest cover and gearing?

27. What is the company's gross margin and is it rising?

28. Have earnings per share risen steadily or have they been volatile?

29. What is the company's net margin, and is it capable of improvement?

30. Has the company generated cash or has its debt been rising?

31. Do all the various divisions or subsidiaries make a profit or does it have loss-makers?

32. Has the company sold any bits recently and, if so, were there write-offs?

33. Does the company have frequent one-off charges or other unusual items in the accounts?

34. Do you consider the company's accounting policies conservative or imprudent?

35. Does it have substantial tangible assets such as property or a lot of intangibles?

36. Does it have any valuable investments or associates?

37. Does it have litigation or other contingent liabilities?

38. How significant are the company's lease and HP commitments?

39. Is it vulnerable to currency fluctuations or commodity price movements?

40. Does the company have overseas operations and are they successful?

41. When were the most recently published results and how good were they?

42. Who are the major shareholders and could the company fall prey to a takeover?

43. Is the company well covered by stockbroking analysts and do they rate it a buy?

44. Has it issued any profit warnings or has it met expectations?

45. Does the company have an order book and, if so, is it strong or poor?

46. Does it report like-for-like sales and, if so, are they positive?

47. What has been the share price performance in the past 12 months?

48. Are the shares liquid and can you buy and sell them relatively easily?

49. Is the company's price/earnings ratio attractive and reasonable relative to similar companies?

50. Is the company's dividend yield attractive and reasonable relative to similar companies?

October 1999

Estate Agents

Amid the wreckage of the London stock market, few sectors have escaped the battering. One group of companies that looks to have been harshly treated are the estate agents. As a profession everyone loves to hate them, but that doesn't mean to say their shares aren't worth buying. Even if the property business goes into a prolonged slowdown, their valuations seem low.

The largest by far is Countrywide Assured Group, with over 800 shops. They specialise in residential property and have fairly big financial services and life assurance divisions. They have net cash and have just published strong results for 2002, with cashflow 113% of profits. While their biggest division, the estate agency business, has shown weakness in recent months, their surveying operations remain strong. They are obviously something of a gamble on the resilience of the housing market, but they do have a diversity of income streams and are not wholly dependent on the London market. While interest rates and unemployment stay low the national housing market will not crash. The shares yield almost 6% and are on a prospective P/E of around six.

The rest of the bunch are smaller and tend to be focused on commercial agency work. Savills is worth around £90 million and has revenues of over £280 million. Again, recent results showed strong growth last year but caution in the outlook for 2003. However, the company increased its dividend by 5% and the shares now yield over 7.5% and stand on a P/E of no more than 6 at 136p. The business derives 40% of its revenues from overseas, and is a demonstration of how UK brands are world leaders in the property profession. The business once more has substantial net cash and a spread of activities, from commercial and residential lettings and sales to auctions, development and investment business, valuation, planning, agricultural consultancy and facilities management. The management insist they have a lean, flexible cost base, enabling them to withstand difficult commercial property markets.

Possibly the cheapest of the lot is DTZ Holdings. The shares languish at 51p, offering a yield of 12% – with a recently maintained dividend. Estimates for the current year to April 2003 have been lowered to about £9 million of profits and 7.5p of earnings – giving a P/E of 6.8. Once more the company has negligible debt – indeed its share price is virtually covered by net current assets. Like most of the agencies, the share register is not controlled, so in theory the business could be bid for. At such bombed out valuations, takeovers or privatisations could well happen.

Perhaps the most speculative of the estate agents is Chesterton International. It is now valued at just £6 million, following a prolonged period of takeover talks and the appointment of a new team of Chief Executive and Finance Director. The business turns over at least £150 million and could probably be debt-free after disposals of various non-core assets. It has a medium-sized facilities management business and the usual range of agency and consultancy services in both residential and commercial property. The financial track record of the business is poor, but there is potential to cut costs and Chesterton is a well-known brand. The shares are a punt on the turnaround abilities of the new executives.

Fitzhardinge plc operates as Colliers CRE, or the old Conrad Ritblat Erdman chartered surveying business. Delancey Estates, controlled by the Ritblat family, own about 37% of the shares. The business is valued at £32 million at 106p and is quoted on AIM. It was only created as a public company last year, so its track record is rather shorter than the other quoted surveyors. It is on a prospective P/E of perhaps 11, and is a highly illiquid share, so perhaps the least attractive stock of the group.

The final quoted player is Hercules Property Services. This owns various agency brands but makes most of its money arranging property insurance for blocks of flats. The shares have collapsed to 74p, valuing it at £13 million. It had sales of £36 million to June 2002. In theory the business will make £8 million of profits this year, and yields over 10%. The market obviously has serious doubts about the business, and the company has £25 million of debt, but even so the price seems low.

Overall the estate agency sector seems as unloved as any, but in most cases the companies concerned seem in reasonable condition. Current prices are discounting very bad news. Are things really that grim?

March 2003

Perception and Reality in Chairmen's Statements

Companies tend to try and put the best light on their results – optimism is after all a necessary ingredient in any business undertaking. Over the years, the Chairman's statement accompanying the preliminary results has become a work of art, putting a positive spin on bad news and playing down the negatives.

In an attempt to help investors gain a better understanding of the painful truth which underlies the gloss, I have provided a running commentary in brackets to the statement recently published by Bullish PLC, a well-known listed company. In this task, I have been much helped by Elderstreet, who publish an excellent little series of interpretive guides to such double-speak.

"Your company is pleased to announce another set of solid figures. *We achieved no increase in sales or profits, but the Board awarded itself a pay rise.* In difficult conditions, we made real progress towards many of our long-term goals. *The market is quite terrible and we were lucky not to go bust: our main goal is to stay in business.* Sales were £165 million and profits before tax £3.2 million. *Since no comparison is given, they must be less than last year's.* Earnings per share rose by 10% to 8p. *The tax charge must have fallen dramatically to achieve that.* As a demonstration of the Board's confidence in the future, we are increasing the dividend by 12%. *We realise we are now a yield stock, and if we don't offer investors some sort of succour they'll sack us.*

Our major division – industrial distribution – was restructured to produce better returns in future. *We fired the entire senior management and sacked half the workforce.* We are confident the new strategy will prove effective over the medium term. *If we all live to a very great age the business might turn around.* I have every confidence in the new team. *They are completely untested and might also have to be replaced.* We have increased research and development spending in order to expand our product offering. *We have no products and desperately lag the competition.* We believe this division is a core business for your group. *It is in decline and for sale to anyone who wants to buy it.*

We have repositioned the other divisions of the group into one division – called Other Products. *These subsidiaries were in chaos and make no sense being merged, but it allows us to kitchen-sink the problems.* There have been certain necessary costs which will lead to savings in the years to come. *Vast investment had to be written off – who knows about next year, let alone beyond that.* Gross margins have been under pressure. *We are making a loss on everything we sell.* Exchange rates and subsidized overseas competitors have made conditions difficult in this division. *Blame everything but management deficiencies.* However, we now have a coherent strategy for this division and prospects are improving. *No one understands what we do, including the senior management.*

Our balance sheet remains strong. *Full of redundant stock, bad debtors, clapped out machines and old buildings.* We enjoy the full support of our bankers. *They have not yet appointed receivers, but we are in intensive care.* Morale across the group is high. *We're looking forward to big pay-offs when we get fired.* Customer relations are excellent. *No one has sued us yet.* We feel sure your company has a great future as an independent entity. *If the group gets bid for I will lose my chauffeur!*

We have established a new internet division to exploit the considerable opportunities on the web, and expect great things from this investment. *To prop up our share price the PR firm said we should mention the internet.*

You may have read about the litigation in which the group is involved. Your Board firmly believes that this action lacks merit and will be defended vigorously. *By the time the case comes to court we'll all have retired, so who cares.*

Prospects for the current year are mixed. *Catastrophe looms, but something will turn up.* We expect to exceed budget in the first six months. *The budget was set ridiculously low – the second six months are going to be an unmitigated disaster.* We also intend to vigorously pursue our acquisition strategy. *Without a deal the company is dead.* As ever, we aim to focus on shareholder value. *Especially the option-holders sitting in the Boardroom.* I personally am committed to building your group into a world-class player in its industry. *I have my eye on a corporate Gulfstream jet.*

Finally, I would like to pay special thanks to the hard-working staff across the group. *Those who we haven't fired owing to our gross incompetence over many years.*"

February 2000

Forestry

I recently read an interview with a highly successful and respected US money manager called Jeremy Grantham, and a particular remark caught my eye. The Boston-based investor mentioned that his favourite asset class was timber, because it was the only low-risk, high-return such asset in existence. He argued that timber is the only commodity that has experienced a steadily rising price for 200 years, 100 years, 50 years, and 10 years. He suggested that it returned an average of about 6.5% from 1910 to 2000, while the yield from US stocks averaged 4.5%. With present low interest rates, a safe return like that is not bad.

Now Mr Grantham is conservative, and pretty bearish about current equity markets. But he does manage $22 billion, so it is worth paying attention to him. And investment in UK forestry provides particular tax benefits for individual British taxpayers that are worth considering. Essentially, the increment in the value of trees is free from tax. There is no income or capital gains tax, and 100% relief from inheritance tax.

There are other positive points about timber as an investment. It offers ownership of a tangible asset that grows naturally. It can be harvested when it suits, since the forest can be withheld. If the price of lumber is poor, then the trees are not cut – and they continue to grow and become more valuable. As it happens, the UK excels at growing and processing softwood timber, and we are one of the world's major consumers and importers of wood. And trees are a growth market. World consumption of wood products is estimated to rise by 1.7% per annum to 2010. Its future as an industrial raw material appears assured.

Meanwhile supply is being increasingly constricted by environmental and conservation issues. Projections suggest the supply of roundwood harvested plantations as opposed to natural forests will rise from around 25% today to 34% by 2010.

Another reason I like the sound of timber as an investment is that it is obscure. Unusual asset classes like timber tend to get overlooked, and are thus more likely to be imperfect markets and give better value to investors.

Yet another selling feature of UK forestry is the fact that both timber and property prices are depressed. Current prices are at just about their lowest ever level in real terms – over 40% below the last peak reached in 1995.

There are some definite negative aspects to forestry as an investment. It is unquestionably a long term play. A minimum time horizon should be five years – in reality the longer the better. Trees become larger and the price per cubic metre increases the more mature the tree is. A realistic time span might be ten to fifteen years. There is limited liquidity, and essentially only occasional opportunities to sell. And costs and commissions seem high to me – both the initial upfront fees to the promoters of forestry investment schemes, and operating costs payable to managers of the forests.

There are various other risks: the trees could suffer premature damage by windthrow, when they fail to develop firm roots to protect against the wind. There are pests and diseases that can attack commercial tree plantations; there is some fire risk; and there is the possible threat of acid rain. But most of these dangers can be insured against, or otherwise covered.

Of course there is another critical factor about trees as an investment. Forestry is environmentally friendly. A friend gave me a marvellous book once called *The Man Who Planted Trees*. It is a simple, short work by a Frenchman called Jean Giono, about a shepherd who spends his life on a mission to reforest the earth. It is a sort of parable about the importance of nature and how to achieve happiness. It is a brilliant reminder of how important trees are in the great scheme of things. We all know trees absorb carbon dioxide, helping to offset possible global warming, and enhance the landscape and provide biodiversity. Perhaps by investing in forestry one can make money, do some good and enjoy some of the intangible returns that The Man Who Planted Trees achieved.

September 2001

Langbar

London is an interesting place. It must be, because an extraordinary array of characters from all over the world choose to come and do business here. They come from Russia, they come from India, they come from China, they come from the Middle East. It might be Greenwich Mean Time, it might be our language, or it might be our tax treatment of non-domiciles. One of the latest attractions is AIM, our stock market for fledgling companies – and easily the most successful such exchange after NASDAQ in the US.

AIM has had an outstanding couple of years. It will welcome 400 new companies this year, more than double the number that joined in 2003, and is on target to raise almost £6 billion – nearly treble the 2003 total. The average daily value of AIM shares traded has risen over six-fold in the last two years. And a major component of AIM's growth has been the increase in foreign listings: over 90 admissions in 2005 alone are by international rather than domestic issuers. For example, in October it listed Beximo Pharmaceuticals from Bangladesh, Energy XXI Acquisition Corporation, registered in Bermuda, DIC Entertainment Holdings from the US, Galapagos, a Belgian biotech company, and two Australian gold mining stocks.

Why has AIM done so well in recent times? I can think of three principal explanations. Firstly, most brokers now charge at least 5% commission on money raised on AIM – significantly higher fees than they used to levy. So it has become much more profitable for the advisors to sponsor flotations on AIM. Secondly, its relatively light regulatory regime means companies can avoid the burden of bureaucracy like Sarbanes-Oxley, which applies in the US. And thirdly, London has become a major centre for hedge funds, many of which are becoming increasingly desperate in their search for outperformance. Some obviously believe AIM's esoteric array of offerings is a solution to their problem.

While the achievements of AIM are to be applauded, this rapid progress has a price. There have been a number of high profile mining disasters, like Regal Petroleum – perhaps only to be expected in such a speculative industry. And I fear another major scandal is erupting around an obscure company called Langbar International – previously known as Crown Corporation. This came to AIM in October 2003, raising $275 million. A majority of the shares were subscribed by Lambert Financial Investments, seemingly a pension fund for retired Israeli soldiers living in South America. The main promoter, Chairman and Chief Executive was a Dr Maurice Rybak. The auditors were 'Gironella Velasco auditores, S.A.' from Barcelona. The company immediately "obtained a number of large scale contracts in South America which it was able to dispose of for a significant profit." These were sold to Lambert, its 60% shareholder. Purportedly the profit from this deal was $280 million, tax free. This meant Crown should have been sitting on over $500 million of cash.

Curiously, by early 2005 the shares had fallen from an issue price of 360p to a low of around 15p, a tiny fraction of the apparent 250p net cash value per share. In the summer of this year Stuart Pearson was appointed Acting Chairman and Chief Executive, and Dr Rybak stepped down. Mr Pearson, an ex-partner of accountants Baker Tilley, set about improving the share price. He re-named the company after his corporate finance boutique which he reversed in for two million shares. He appointed Arden Partners as brokers, who received 3.12 million warrants to subscribe for shares at 35p each. Arden have since exercised the warrants and sold the underlying shares. Mr Pearson also appointed a new board director, raised £4 million from a placing at 48p with various institutions, and gave an interview covering a full page with this newspaper. Things seemed on the up and the shares recovered to over 90p at one point.

Unfortunately in October there was bad news. On the 11th the shares were suspended, despite Langbar being in the middle of an all paper bid for an AIM stock called Real Affinity. Prior to the suspension Dr Rybak had been busy selling over four million shares in the company he founded. The corporate detectives Kroll Associates were appointed to try to find Langbar's cash deposits of £365 million, meant to be held in Banco do Brasil and ABN Amro. They announced last week that they have not been able to verify the existence of the "any of the relevant assets at any time in the company's history" – and indeed it "appears likely that the company has been subject to a serious fraud." The police have been informed, and no doubt the Serious Fraud Office will get involved. Whether the company will recover any assets remains to be seen.

Cases like this demonstrate why investors should take great care with overseas AIM stocks, and only risk funds they can comfortably afford to lose.

November 2005

Why to Buy a Share

A little while ago I wrote a column giving a list of reasons to avoid certain shares. I think it is now time to put forward the opposite list, one which highlights positive characteristics to look for in shares you are considering buying.

These pointers are not necessarily all textbook justifications – they are simply some of the factors I like. In isolation, none is enough – you need a pattern of several such indicators before taking the plunge.

In essence, I am by nature a value investor: I like to focus my investments; I like out-of-favour situations with takeover potential; I like neglected smaller companies; and I like investing in situations I can understand.

• Neglect from the analyst community, which can lead to sharp undervaluations stemming from ignorance and lack of interest from institutions. Too much analyst coverage can lead to growth shares becoming overvalued. Analysts frequently get things wrong anyway.

• A price to sales ratio of less than one, and ideally less than 0.5. If the price to sales ratio is less than 0.2 (in other words, it is valued at 20% of annual sales or less) for a standard commercial business, then this is a very attractive feature.

• No controlling shareholders – especially not on the Board. This means the company could be taken over. This is particularly important in the current climate, when corporate private equity buyers are so active.

• A large depreciation charge, so that the EBITDA (earnings before interest, tax, depreciation and amortization) figure is much higher than the operating profit figure. Occasionally you find companies where the EBITDA is more than twice the operating profit – such a business might be an ideal leveraged buyout candidate.

• Ambitious new management coming into an underperforming

and lowly-rated company. Frequently the market can take a while to pick up on such important changes. Try to find out the track record of the new boss and their plans.

• Recovery stocks which have had just one horrible year, but possess a strong underlying business which will bounce back rapidly. Often the market overreacts when good companies disappoint, and this oversold condition can create a buying opportunity.

• Companies in sectors with plenty of consolidation and corporate activity. Look for companies which have stumbled which occupy market niches where there are likely to be buyers. Frequently trade buyers will pay big prices for marginally profitable companies simply to eliminate competition and increase market share.

• Shares which have fallen by at least 50% from their 12 month high. This is the opposite of momentum investing: it is contrarian investing. It involves picking stocks others hate, and looking in the bargain basement rather than buying obvious, highly-regarded shares.

• Shares at a discount to tangible net assets. Even though investors place much less emphasis on physical assets than they used to, if a business trades below the true worth of its buildings, plant, and net working capital, then it can always be broken up for liquidation purposes and provide a profit.

• Shares trading at a low price-to-free-cash-flow ratio. Free cash flow means the surplus after tax, capital expenditure and working capital requirements. This cash is available to pay dividends, buy back shares, or repay debt. Again, companies with minimal capital expenditure and working capital needs are likely to attract a bid if they fall out of favour.

• Companies with a great formula which can be duplicated easily. By this I mean 'roll-out' type situations, where a particular product, service or outlet can be spread geographically and the economics of the individual unit are attractive.

- Steady, intelligent buying of the company's shares by the Board in material amounts. Worthwhile purchases by executive Directors are the best guides.

- Conservative accounts. Companies that understate their profits and assets can be attractive. Look for revaluations which have not be incorporated into the accounts or over-prudent write-offs or depreciation policies.

- Companies in industries with which you are familiar. Play to your personal strengths: if you have particular understanding of a certain trade, then use your knowledge to back the right players at the right times. This works best when you buy a bombed-out situation knowing the underlying qualities of the company.

- High-yielding shares. Although many investors shun dividends as irrelevant, a high yield in itself normally indicates an unpopular share. And getting a healthy income while you wait for the takeover bid or the rerating will help your returns.

- Look at gross and net margins. Buy companies with respectable margins which can at least be maintained, or companies which have temporarily depressed margins which will revert to healthy levels quickly.

- Remember there are no perfect companies or absolute values. Most of the time it is better to be invested than not, so do not look for miracle stocks – find things that are sufficiently cheap, get to understand them and then take meaningful positions and be patient.

May 2001

A *Really* Ethical Portfolio

The well-meaning pension fund trustee began:

"The time has come to examine our share portfolio to see if our investments can do good as well as make money. We must be ruthless, and expunge any shares in companies which pursue policies in conflict with a happier, fairer world of sustainable growth. I propose that we conduct this survey of the London stock market sector by sector, so that we may focus our funds on those industries which are untainted."

And so he started the process: "*Aerospace & Defence* – clearly quite unacceptable. All these companies make arms or products which go into weapons of destruction. So no shares in this sector are permissible."

He continued: "*Automobiles* – most of these companies make polluting vehicles which are destroying the countryside and ruining the environment. Others make arms or components which go into arms. Best to steer clear."

Next: "*Banks* – obviously a dangerous area. Virtually all these organisations lend to arms companies, tobacco and alcohol firms or trade with repressive regimes. The safest policy is to avoid all banks, which mostly exploit the poor and Third World anyhow."

He was getting into his stride now. "The next sector is *Beverages*. It sounds harmless enough, but in reality these are all essentially brewers or distillers of intoxicating liquor. Thus they are a definite no-go area."

"The next sector is *Chemicals*. This is very worrying. It even sounds unethical. All these type of companies do huge damage to the environment. Even if they say they take care of the waste they might be lying. We cannot risk it. Exclude them for the list."

"What is next? Ah – *Construction and Building Materials*. This is difficult. It is important to encourage house building to help the homeless. But most of these builders just build for the rich, and anyway they often use greenfield sites and wreck the environment. And the building material suppliers create huge waste problems. Safest to leave them out."

"*Distributors* come next. Some of these seem safe enough. I don't trust the car dealers though. *Diversified Industrials* could be anything – too risky to chance it. *Electricity* seems all right – but probably most of them use electricity generated from nuclear power – oh dear."

"*Electronic & Electrical Equipment* – I wonder how many supply the military. The same goes for *Engineering & Machinery*. *Food & Drug Retailers* are pursuing rip-off pricing and cheating the consumer – I cannot back them. *Food Producers & Processors* – they mistreat animals and exploit poor countries. Beyond the pale. *Forestry & Paper* – they are reputed to be an ecological nightmare and quite unsuitable"

The speaker was becoming a little desperate in his search for a perfectly ethical portfolio. He reeled off sector names: "*Health and Pharmaceuticals* – no, the drug companies endorse vivisection. *Household Goods & Textiles* – no, they exploit prison and child labour in dictatorships. *Insurance* – no, they are conspiring with the tobacco companies to deny responsibility for millions of deaths, so as to continue peddling their evil wares."

It was all rather restrictive and depressing for the trustees. Everyone wanted to do the right thing, but so many companies just didn't seem very responsible. What on earth could one invest in and still feel you were contributing to a better, healthier planet, rather than destroying the earth? What was it about the profit motive which made companies so wicked?

The trustee was close to despair: "*Mining*? Hardly. *Restaurants, Pubs & Brewing*? Not exactly. *Media* – much of that is pornography. *Oil & Gas* – huge despoilers of land and sea. *Tobacco*? A joke, surely. *Water*? They are all meant to be environmental villains."

He sighed in a resigned way, and said: "The only thing for it is to forget shares all together, and just keep the money in the bank." But as he said this he suddenly thought: the bank was probably funding wars, and helping companies which are cruel to animals...

September 1999

A Bitter Pill from My Vet

I have been a shareholder in an AIM quoted company called VDC for some time. Its main business is the distribution of drugs to vets and it has sales of about £90m and a market value of about £20m. Since April 26th it has been under siege from a smallish public company called Genus.

I find the behaviour of the board of VDC, who are paid to generate shareholder value, little short of outrageous.

Genus have made an unsolicited offer to the value of 190p a share in cash for VDC, which values it at about £21m.

The shares at VDC have been much higher in the past, but VDC made a terrible acquisition of a business called Procare, a couple of years ago, which has substantially destroyed the shareholder value.

The underlying business of VDC is sound, but the management insisted on diversifying and the group lost its way and was derated.

The sensible response to hostile cash takeovers is to both negotiate with the bidder for a higher offer, and search for alternative buyers who might be prepared to pay more.

Instead of this, the directors of VDC have entered into an extraordinary arrangement.

Rather than secure another purchaser for VDC, they have agreed to buy a third smallish quoted group called Lawrence, which is also involved in the supply of products to the animal health industry.

Unquestionably, the agreed offer for Lawrence by VDC is good news for Lawrence shareholders. The offer for £30.8m in shares and cash represents a 22 per cent premium over the pre-bid price of Lawrence shares.

It values Lawrence at more than 15 times earnings, and allows the Chief Executive and his family to both take out cash of almost £8m and emerge with 23 per cent of the shares of the enlarged group after the deal. Lawrence also becomes chief executive of the new group.

Thus, this odd transaction is really a reverse takeover for no premium.

Control is passed to Lawrence, and VDC shareholders are being offered no cash, but see their shareholders significantly diluted. VDC's board argues that Genus is valuing the ongoing VDC business at only 10.6 times historic earnings. But VDC is now proposing to dilute its own share capital by 100 per cent and buy Lawrence at a substantially higher p/e than its own, while surrendering control and increasing its debt levels.

VDC shareholders will also be left paying the fees for the VDC defence, and the merger with Lawrence (on both sides).

The purchase of Lawrence could probably be organised as a pure merger, which would have given rise to no acquired goodwill.

But because of the cash element of the deal, the goodwill will amount to about £20m – or a £1m write-off every year for the next 20 years!

This has all the hallmarks of a rushed deal hatched out of a desperate desire not to sell to Genus, rather than a desire to really get known value for VDC shareholders now.

The board of VDC says that they have had outline discussions with Lawrence about a merger for some time, but these must have happened since March 11, since the chairman of VDC had bought shares in his company on that date.

Given the circumstances, the Lawrence deal seems massively one-sided against VDC – but it is amazing the lengths to which boards will go in order to resist hostile takeovers. I have never met or spoken with Genus, and know little about them except that they specialise in bull semen (that is not a joke).

But that is not the point: they have the cash.

It has taken their offer to spur the VDC management into action, and their response has been one of the most self-destructive bid defences I have seen in a long time.

Although I am not a large shareholder in VDC, I think I own more shares than any individual board member, so perhaps I shouldn't be so surprised at their actions.

I am surprised that their advisers, Beeson Gregory, felt able to recommend the defence.

Substantial extra costs have now been incurred by VDC over this folly, when VDC should have been persuading Genus to offer more for an agreed deal.

If the Genus offer lapses, I believer the VDC share price will cave in. VDC shareholders should vote down the crazy Lawrence deal at the extraordinary meeting.

They should press their board to get a better cash offer, or they should simply sell their VDC shares in the market, since they are trading above the value of the Genus offer.

For me, keeping VDC shares with any of the present board is not an option.

May 1999

Give these Market Myths a Miss

I have written before about "rules" one can apply to the business of investing. In truth, trying to arrange order out of the chaos that is the stock market is not as simple as always applying a set of fixed parameters.

But behavioural psychology shows that we frequently believe the use of systems can help us predict the future. This means that bogus and dangerous tendencies turn up which are unreliable, but tend to give investors comfort – and so may corrupt their decision making. Among these market fallacies are the following:

- *Low-priced shares are cheap shares*
  Do not believe a penny stock is cheap per se. True share value relates to items such as sales, assets, earnings and dividends on a per share basis – what matters most is the ratio of these items to the share price, not the absolute share price. A penny share can be very expensive and a highly priced share very cheap. It is extraordinary how many investors do not realise this.

- *The leaders and experts must be right*
  Just because the top professionals and gurus say something does not mean it is correct. Blindly following the crowd will not necessarily produce the best, or even adequate returns. At the end of last year many funds and analysts were dismissive of smaller companies and touted the major, global stocks. Yet so far this year the smaller company indices in the UK are up almost 10 times as much as the major market indices.

- *Buzzwords and new terminology mean an industry is exciting and a good investment*
  Do not be fooled by lots of mumbo-jumbo. The internet is stuffed full of such jargon – everything from portals, ISPs, protocols, NAPs, hosting, ISDN and so on. Quite often such vocabulary is adopted to reduce the understanding of outsiders, and perhaps justify a higher valuation. If plain English cannot explain what the business does, is it an appropriate investment?

- *More information means you make better investments*
  The quantity of data available about quoted companies is far greater than ever before. But sometimes this vast weight of facts can help to confuse rather than simplify. Investment is about making two decisions, buying and selling. Most of the important facts regarding a stock are plainly visible. An overload of spreadsheets and industry statistics will only clutter the picture.

- *Companies where you have met the management are better than companies where you have not*
  We are all human. We tend to trust and like people we have met over the unknown. It is natural to overvalue things where we have had personal contact. But just because you have spoken with management does not mean the company is sound, or even that you really know it better than a company you have only studied from afar.

- *You can judge the future based on the immediate past*
  We tend to rely overly on recent facts and extrapolate accordingly, and fail to take in the big picture. In general, investors believe they know more than they really do, and overrate their investing abilities. Especially in bull markets, when many shares are rising, even fools imagine they are brilliant and they become over-confident. The laws of probability suggest that over time many investors will make money. This does not mean they are clever – it may well just mean they have been lucky.

- *There are risk-free, profit-making opportunities in the stockmarket*
  All shares can fall as well as rise. In theory you can lose 100 per cent of your investment if a company goes bust. All investors who outperform know about risk and losses. In fact, most investors take too few risks: experiments have shown that most people are risk-averse, even where the likely gain outweighs the likely loss. For most people, the fear of loss is greater than the desire for gain. If you want to get rich by investing, be prepared for risk.

- *New issues are a sure thing*
  During bull markets flotations tend to do well. But extensive US research has shown that over a five year view investing in new issues leads to underperformance against the market. Similar studies in the UK are less conclusive. You should be just as discriminating with new issues as other shares. What they have going for them is that they are new, and being sold hard by the sponsors. But they are not always cheap, nor are they always good companies.

- *There is only one winning investment style*
  Just as there are various routes to wealth, so there are many different ways to invest. Simply because Warren Buffett has become the richest investor on earth does not mean he has the only valid approach to the stock market. I would even go so far as to say that this methodology is quite wrong in many respects for an amateur investor with a small to medium sized share portfolio. Evolve your own approach after testing a variety of methodologies.

The investing game is full of fantasy for several reasons. We all fail to learn sufficiently from experience; we are lazy and do not do enough homework; and we let emotions overcome logic. Constant reminders such as the above can help us improve our performance.

September 1999

Ten-Baggers

One of the best books of modern times about investing was published in 1989 and is called *One Up On Wall Street*. It was written by a clever fund manager at Fidelity called Peter Lynch, and it introduced me to the concept of 'Ten-Baggers' – the Holy Grail of investing.

Ten-baggers are shares where you make ten times your money. I believe the phrase is derived from baseball. Such opportunities are rare and wonderful things, and can turn an entire portfolio around. I have been fortunate enough over the last 15 years to be involved in a few such situations – PizzaExpress, Topps Tiles, and Abacus Recruitment among them.

There tend to be some common characteristics among such winners. The businesses all operate in growth industries, and the company in question must be able to grow the top line. No-one ever made a ten-fold return on a pure margin improvement, or on a cost-cutting story with no sales growth. Turnarounds are however, a rich source of ten-baggers. For these to work, one's timing has to be immaculate, and the underlying business has to be sound – just desperately unloved by the stock market. Those two astonishing retail recovery stories, Next and French Connection, come to mind: both have been ten-baggers for those who bought at the bottom in the early 1990s. Recessions and downturns will throw up such opportunities – decent firms with temporary problems which can be cured.

Such returns need patience – a hedge fund that churns its holdings every few months will never enjoy a ten-bagger. And therein lies the greatest danger: selling too early to enjoy the 1000% gain. When you have doubled or trebled your money, it is so tempting to cash in your profits. It must have been tempting in the early 1950s to take profits on Glaxo shares, just a few years after their 1947 flotation; or do the same for Tesco – floated in the same year; or sell Racal in the late 1960s, after its 1961 market debut – decades before it spun off Vodafone. Yet each of those three shares rewarded patient investors with epic performance over many decades – all twenty-baggers at least – not even allowing for dividend income!

One of the great advantages that private equity enjoys is that it is forced to take a reasonably long-term view, and so is usually unable to rush for the exit at the first opportunity. Venture capital's other edge over quoted investors is debt: gearing in successful situations always amplifies the return to equity-holders. Typically buy-outs have structures where 70% of the capital is borrowed; quoted companies probably have the reverse capitalisation, with equity providing three-quarters of the funding. And as ever in investing, stick to your own sphere of competence: buy what you understand.

A good source of ten-baggers has been privatisations. Of the 43 public sector companies floated in London, at least four have returned more than ten times their issue price: Associated British Ports, Amersham, BP and Forth Ports. Proof, I suppose, that governments tend to sell state assets cheaply to the private sector – or, perhaps, that such organisations thrive out of public ownership. While the UK has few such businesses left to flog off, there are a number of countries such as France and Turkey which have active privatisation programmes where there might just be ten-baggers waiting to be discovered.

Indeed the UK is a mature economy, and therefore finding new sectors – and stocks – experiencing sustained, rapid growth is harder than ever. It may well be that the most exciting investments are overseas in emerging economies which are expanding quickly. Luckily capital markets like AIM are attracting dozens of foreign companies looking to raise money, so British investors do not necessarily need to buy shares quoted on overseas exchanges. But the usual rules apply: look for real companies with competent management and a proven business model. You won't find a ten-bagger among much of the over-hyped, speculative froth that comes to AIM: search for the solid operation with decent fundamentals and a minimum quality of earnings.

Very few acquisition-led vehicles are ten-baggers. Management in such firms focus on doing deals rather than organically growing their core business. This can produce reasonable returns, but rarely delivers the stellar, long-run performance that can come from a strong business franchise in an attractive niche. And balance sheets matter: growth requires funding, and companies that forever issue equity dilute their stock performance.

So good luck in your search for the next blockbuster. It may well be an obscure, neglected company currently: the secret is to spot the potential.

May 2004

Selling Signals

The starting point for analysis of a company is usually its industry sector and markets. Once such broad investigations have been completed, then you should examine the annual report. In this document there are a number of indicators which are not industry specific, but can still be valuable danger signals. Over the years I have been told of many different negative signs to watch out for in a public company. None on their own should justify the sale of a share, but if a company collects a combination of perhaps ten or more serious minus points then I think you might carefully consider whether you should remain a shareholder – even if you like the sector. My list includes the following:

The Board

- Several Directors related to each other;
- Two or fewer executive Directors;
- Two or more knighthoods or similar ennobled non-executives;
- An average age of over 55;
- Salaries rising every year even when profits drop;
- The Chief Executive or Chairman holding less than 25% by value of their annual salary in shares in the company;
- Chauffeurs/First Class Travelling/Company houses or flats/Wimbledon boxes/grouse shoots etc;
- Service contracts of more than two years;
- The non-executive Chairman paid more than £100,000;
- More than one photograph of the Chairman or Chief Executive in the annual report;
- No Chief Executive or Managing Director, just an Executive Chairman;
- Annual general meetings held at awkward times on difficult dates in obscure places;

- The Company's lawyer or merchant banker serving as a non-executive Director;
- High turnover of Directors – especially Finance Directors;
- Large share sales by key executive Directors.

The Accounts

- Repeated 'one-off' items which would have reduced profits;
- More than three lending bankers;
- Very posh brokers and merchant banks acting for smaller companies;
- Vague accounting policies regarding matters such as depreciation, leases and research and development;
- Growing earnings by reducing the tax charge every year;
- An annual report which completely fails to explain what the company does;
- Too much irrelevant sponsorship of junket stuff like horse or motor racing;
- Pointless acquisitions designed to act as a smokescreen;
- Despite being profitable, the business never generates cash;
- Growing sales to disguise declining margins;
- Capitalising expenses as assets on a large scale;
- Repeatedly paying an uncovered dividend to prop up the share price;
- Very high audit and professional fees;
- Regular sales of fixed assets at a book loss;
- Majority controlled by overseas shareholders;
- Extensive and regular related party transactions;
- Reporting figures late and on a Friday afternoon;

- So many acquisitions that they never stand still long enough for you to analyse how the underlying business is doing;
- No real core activity;
- Consistently earning a poor return on capital.

These points are about two issues: (a) Are the right people running the business? and (b) Are they window-dressing the numbers? Inevitably, there will be occasional exceptional companies which do well despite breaking lots of the above rules. But generally, if a company fails many of the above tests then it is likely to underperform.

December 2002

Regus

I reckon that Mark Dixon must be a very clever fellow. He's the chap who cycles to work and has built up Regus Business Centres plc, which is about to become worth around a billion pounds when it floats on the London Stock Exchange. And Mr Dixon is soon to be a dollar billionaire, since he still owns over 80% of the company. He's done it all in ten years in one of the oldest games in town, the property world.

Now one or two of my property chums are completely baffled by the valuation of Regus. They have been running traditional property companies for decades, gradually building their asset base and rental streams, while developing new buildings. They own freehold structures and have tenants with strong covenants on long leases, and they possess skill in finding sites, obtaining planning permissions, constructing properties and letting them successfully. Yet these companies are almost always valued by the stock market at a discount to net book value and on reasonable dividend yields. These stocks are seen as fairly safe but dull.

Regus on the other hand offers a heady mix of the dynamic and global. It is signing office leases all over the world like a dervish. It doesn't appear to develop or own any of its buildings – it just tarts them up and finds very short-term tenants, who are charged very high rents. While its pre-new money valuation on flotation is likely to be about £750 million, at 31 December 1998 it only had about £25 million of net worth. In that year it also only had £112 million of sales, and lost over £11 million. According to projections by Morgan Stanley, it is likely to lose over £42 million this year, and carry on losing money after depreciation until at least 2002.

Why Mark Dixon is spectacularly clever is that in August 1998 he sold 17.5% of the business to Bankers Trust (now Deutsche Bank) and various powerful interests for $100 million. This underwrote a valuation then of £350 million and brought on board influential allies who could help package a flotation at an appropriately rich price. The great stock shifting machine is now in full gear, with Merrill Lynch, Morgan Stanley and Deutsche Bank all in maximum selling mode. The whole carnival is in motion: bulky analyst circulars, smooth PR firms, and classy presentations.

And they have managed to convince the FTSE Actuaries that Regus should be classified under Support Services – not the property/real estate sector. This means Regus is being compared to Serco and Capita, two superstar service stocks, both now on price earnings multiples to make your eyes water, rather than boring stuff like MEPC, Land Securities or British Land. Regus is to join the rating heaven of 'outsourcing'. The fact is that when Serco and Capita originally went public they were valued on conventional p/e ratios, rather than mumbo-jumbo-like multiples of revenue.

I am not sure that the barriers to entry are high for the Regus business. A well funded competitor could quite quickly sign office leases in many of the cities in which Regus operate. It could then undercut the Regus terms, which are extortionate; after all, rents are only a quarter of Regus's costs, suggesting its tenants pay four times as much for their space as Regus! Plenty of room for discounting there. Since tenant agreements with Regus are short term, they could quite quickly switch to alternative suppliers. Indeed, the business of Regus is not even new: there have been serviced office companies for many years – there are even quite large international players already, like HQ Global Workplace. Much of this belongs to CarrAmerica Realty, a New York Stock Exchange listed company valued at less than Regus will be, available for 16 times earnings, growing rapidly with $700 million of sales, standing at 85% of book value and which actually owns most of its buildings!

Regus uses some racy accounting policies. 93% of its fixed assets are furniture and fittings, yet it writes these off over seven years. They must be tough chairs and carpets. It capitalises start-up costs of new centres and amortises them over three years. It opened many of its best UK sites in the early 1990s, when landlords were desperate for tenants and rents were low. Such bargain deals are no longer available, and upwards-only rent reviews will correct these anomalies. Moreover, Regus has a focus in the UK where traditionally lease structures are inflexible – in other countries the Regus model may prove less successful.

The sponsoring brokers suggest 'discounted cash flow analysis is the best available valuation basis'. This is presumably because more mundane methods such as net worth, dividend yield or the price-earnings ratio would value the business at very little. Clearly I am too stupid and backwards-looking to truly understand a pioneering situation like Regus or the basis for its valuation. I just keep thinking of the story of the Emperor and his new clothes...

September 1999

This business has experienced an extraordinary rollercoaster ride since I first wrote about it. It managed to go public in October 2000 and raised £239 million. It then fell into losses of £110 million in 2001 and worse the following year, when it was forced to place its US business in Chapter 11 and sell a majority of its UK business to Alchemy. But Mark Dixon, the resilient founder, pulled the business round and in recent years its fortunes have recovered miraculously. It now owns once more both its US and UK operations and achieved profits of £33 million in the six months to 31st December 2006 alone – a remarkable turnaround.

PartyGaming

Twenty years ago, as a lowly analyst at Kleinwort Benson, I suggested the firm sponsor the flotation of a trade and adult magazine publisher I had come across. My very grand bosses though this type of client was 'inappropriate' for such a posh merchant bank, and turned the business down. How times have changed. Today the same bank is acting as sole sponsor to the highly ambitious IPO of PartyGaming, one of the least attractive new issues I can remember.

It is quite obvious why the business is going public. The owners want to sell some of their shares – for a great deal of money. The business does not need cash, or to issue new shares to make acquisitions. It has no debt to repay, or major capital expenditure needs. So the shares being sold to the public are coming from the founders, who probably understand the risks and rewards rather better than any investors buying shares. And who can blame the four mysterious offshore owners for cashing in? They hope to secure a valuation of up to $10 billion – for a business that had revenues of just £84 million in 2003, and only started running poker sites four years ago. Just to put it in context, this valuation would be a greater market capitalisation than Boots, or Sainsbury's or British Airways – each of which have sales of many billions and have been going at least 50 years.

Life tells one that what goes up very quickly tends to come down the same way. The online poker phenomenon is the most glaring investment bubble the market has seen in a long time. Not only PartyGaming is coming to the London Stock Exchange – so are Empire Online and 888.com, by all accounts. Sportingbet's acquisition last year of Paradise Poker, a rival to PartyPoker, has encouraged this feeding frenzy. It commands a price/earnings multiple of 20 or so – very high for what is clearly a fashion business and subject to a host of technological and legal threats, from worries about money laundering to concerns over computer hackers.

Over 80% of PartyGaming's business is in the US. Yet the whole legality of internet gambling there is questionable. The Department of Justice says that online poker breaches the Wire Wager Act, which forbids gambling across state lines. Various states have specific laws prohibiting online betting. Already the authorities have stopped major media owners from carrying online poker adverts, and many banks decline credit card transactions from gambling sites. If the business grows – the whole basis for the sky-high valuations of these companies – I suspect the powerful and well-connected established gaming companies in the US will either launch their own, well-funded online poker sites – or lobby to encourage the authorities to enforce legislation and help shut down the big internet poker firms. Either way, the high-profile IPO of PartyGaming will not have escaped the attention of the US government and major American gaming firms.

Currently PartyGaming enjoys net income margins of 58% on its commission revenue. Experience suggests such extraordinary profitability is unsustainable in a capitalist system. No other FTSE firm makes margins even close – because such margins don't last. None of the online poker firms has special patents or long-established brands or proprietary technology – the barriers to entry for this sort of business are remarkably low. Loyalty among online gamblers is almost non-existent. Very little capital is needed to build online businesses. As more entrepreneurs become aware of the profits in this game, the number of big poker websites will boom relentlessly, and the poker players will get spread among them. New entrants will offer incentives and undercut the established sites, who will then be forced to spend money to remain competitive.

Another question for PartyGaming is why float here? It is registered in Gibraltar and does most of its business in the US – its owners are all foreign and most of their staff are based in India – it pays no tax in Britain. It can't float in New York because no US bank will get involved and US investors will probably be unable to buy the shares. Rumours even suggest that few of the four founders will serve on the board – and none will serve as Chief Executive or Chairman, who are both very recent recruits.

Inevitably, an elaborate public relations machine has kicked in to try to ensure the IPO is a success. Huge money is at stake, so armies of advisors will make every effort with the media and analysts to 'accentuate the positive, eliminate the negative' – as the song goes. Unfortunately for PartyGaming, the new issue market is in a bad way, and I predict the price will be slashed or the flotation will be pulled.

June 2005

Amazingly the flotation got away in the summer of 2005 at 130p a share. Within months the stock was below the issue price, but the true collapse came in September 2006, when US regulators launched a serious crackdown on 'illegal' online gambling. PartyGaming's shares tumbled to as low as 26p, and currently trade a little above that. The business remains profitable and has net cash, but its future is uncertain.

The Loser's Game, the Winner's Curse and Freud

Investment professionals often assert that they buy and sell shares based on scientific principles, but such a belief ignores the psychology of the markets. The superiority complexes of many such investment pros helps explain why they tend, as a whole, to underperform the market. In many cases they have failed to analyse why their funds are beaten by index or tracker funds. Perhaps analysing their emotions is harder than analysing accounts. They could do worse than read some of the writings of Dr Sigmund Freud of Vienna, who said: "Psychoanalysis warns us to abandon the unfruitful factors of fate and has taught us regularly to discover the cause of neurosis." In the meantime, one can identify a few specific errors that crop up frequently.

The Loser's Game is a phenomenon identified by Dr Simon Ramo and expounded by Charles D. Ellis. It is derived from observations about tennis, which suggest that bad players lose by trying too hard to play winning shots. Translating this into the world of finance, the theory suggests that professional investors underperform the market because they try too hard to beat the market. Thanks to dealing spreads, commissions and so forth, all their hectic activity is mostly a waste of time, since they tend to deliver worse returns than passive funds. With their need for liquidity and scale, trying to find anomalous valuations in larger stocks and out-invest their peers has become increasingly difficult. It is, of course, only human nature for a professional investor to believe his own intellectual efforts will outsmart the competition; but for the majority this policy will inevitably fail.

The Winner's Curse is another concept derived from behavioural psychology. It concerns investors who participate in auctions, such as private equity houses bidding for prime buy-out deals, or contested public company takeovers with rival bidders. Studies indicate that in many such settings the highest bidder will pay too much and be "cursed" with a disappointing deal. Such irrational behaviour occurs because bidders take account of other possible buyers, rather than ignoring competing bids and paying only what the assets are worth. The emotional importance of winning overwhelms the arguments in favour of paying a sensible price.

Another common mistake made by many investors is to become convinced that something is true because they want it to be true. They decide that a share will soon double because they want it to double. They are victims of the Will to Believe. They need to disentangle their emotions from their investments, and remember that a share does not know you own it.

A powerful motivating force in markets is a disproportionate aversion to loss. Studies of human behaviour have shown that most investors will avoid the risk of loss, even when it is outweighed by the likelihood of overall gain. Thus respondents will prefer a sure £30,000 to an 80% chance of £50,000. This preference may partly reflect a lack of understanding of probabilities, but it also shows how people place too much value on apparent certainty. Behaviour like this helps explain the very high price/earnings multiples commanded by companies with supposedly reliable earnings growth. A related behaviour pattern is called the endowment effect, whereby investors require much more to give up an object than they would be willing to pay to acquire it. This demonstrates itself in the way shareholders ask for huge premiums in takeovers, which they would not be willing to pay themselves.

Yet another bias in human thinking which leads to investment errors is in the making and judging of forecasts. Investment decisions are normally based on forecasts, but many of these projections are prepared with in-built errors thanks to recurring psychological bias. For example, (a) most profit forecasts tend to give too much emphasis to recent data and ignore historical trends; (b) investors take too seriously forecasts inferred from small samples of data that seem to manifest a pattern; and (c) most forecasting assumes far more stability than is likely in the real world of business. Overall this leads to too much faith in prospective earnings models, and disappointment when such predictions are not met.

I believe the best investors know their own emotions well and study investor behaviour carefully when considering share purchases and sales. They probably also research the fundamentals of companies, industries and economies too, and then combine the disciplines of psychology and financial analysis to achieve the best results. To ignore either aspect of the investment process would be wrong but to achieve the correct balance takes rare talent.

January 1999

Is the Neuer Markt a Giant Ramp?

What has been the best performing stock market in the world in the last two years? You might be tempted to say Nasdaq, driven by many fabulous internet stocks and high tech giants like Microsoft and Intel. But you would be wrong. By far and away the most successful market in the world since its launch on 10th March 1997 has been Frankfurt's Neuer Markt. It has risen by over 175% since its start two years ago.

This phenomenon was created by the Deutsche Borse to raise capital for innovative companies in fast-growing industries like telecommunications, biotechnology and multimedia. It is apparently a "securities segment of absolutely prime quality". It now has 100 listed companies and a mind-blowing market value of nearly $50 billion. The average historic price/earnings multiple of its constituent stocks is a hairy 42, but this is only encouraging more companies to seek to float. 50 more stocks are expected to go public on the Neuer Markt before the end of 1999.

The soaring prices and rush of new issues contrasts with the historical experience of the German stock market. In the ten years prior to the formation of the Neuer Markt, there were an average of just 17 new listings a year in Germany, despite the fact it has by far Europe's largest economy. In 1999 so far there have already been over 60 initial public offerings – quite the opposite of the barren new issue market in the UK. Traditionally German firms grew using bank debt and retained earnings, and venture capital was hard to raise. Now there are over 150 venture capital outfits in Germany, and many are looking for mechanisms to realise their investments. Moreover, the equity bug has truly caught on among the Germany public, despite the sluggish economy there. Suddenly fortunes are being made overnight by dealing in speculative shares or by floating companies – a pornography business recently went public on a P/E of over 40.

The Neuer Markt boom contrasts with the sad state of AIM, which despite having around 310 stocks trading has a market capitalisation of just $7 billion. The stagnant new issue market in the UK and the reluctance of many institutional investors to participate in AIM means it is in grave danger of going the way of the 3rd Market and the USM. It would be a great shame if the AIM experiment failed, since the London Stock Exchange has tried hard to make it work. But AIM has become cluttered with too much rubbish, and the typical issue is not high quality. Virtually the only source of ready money for AIM new issues are Venture Capital Trusts, which invest with tax-break money, but only in qualifying situations. I have a suspicion new e-markets will replace AIM for high tech issues, the key sector in emergent company investing.

The German stock exchange deliberately set fairly high standards for entrants: companies have to report quarterly and publish announcements in both German and English and use US accounting principles; they have to have two sponsoring brokers providing research and making markets; and they must ensure at least half the money raised in the flotation is for the benefit of the company, rather than selling shareholders. These requirements are all very clever: quarterly reporting is important in the fast-moving world of high tech; publishing in English encourages US and UK investors and companies to get involved; the involvement of two investment banks helps provide balance; and the final rule discourages promoters from going public to cash out straight away. And finally, the official listing fees are modest by London standards: the initial admission fee payable to the Neuer Markt is about one fifteenth of the Full List fees in London.

But it may be that the Neuer Markt has been far too successful. Many issuers have smallish free floats of shares and trading in them can be volatile. Lots of private punters crowding into the shares are complete amateurs who have never known stocks to disappoint. The rollercoaster ride of the net mania in the US and recent sharp falls of net stocks shows how dangerous such heady valuations can be for the inexperienced.

The raw function of stock markets is to supply equity funding for the risky undertakings of industry. Clearly this new German exchange in achieving this. Indeed, it is also helping the growth of venture capital itself by providing exits and realisations for the better venture investments – so that the cash can be recycled. But like so much activity in financial markets, success has overshot and valuations on the Neuer Markt are plainly excessive. These extremes are attracting even US internet companies to float in Germany – this has to be a serious sell signal. The correction in Frankfurt will be painful and shocking, but I hope the Neuer Markt survives and continues to attract companies and money.

June 1999

In fact the Neuer Markt closed in late 2002 following the bursting of the dotcom bubble. AIM meanwhile has gone from strength to strength, and is now the world's most dynamic stock exchange for growth companies.

Why Stock Markets Always Kill The Ones They Love The Most

When companies need to raise funds for new business projects, traditionally they obtain equity from a stock exchange. This formation of new capital for new commercial undertakings is the most important economic purpose served by such a securities market. That is why the process of going public is significant. But very often the market has a love/hate relationship with any company, and the seeds of many corporate downfalls are sown right at the beginning when the firm first debuts on the exchange.

Many institutional funds are net investors in the equity market – they need to buy more than they sell. So they require a steady stream of new share issues. Investment banks and brokers want fresh corporate business to generate fees and excitement. New businesses can spark interest among the investment community and publicity for the underwriter – everyone courts them. For most would-be new issues, there is a beauty parade of brokers who promise great things, as salesmen do.

Meanwhile companies go public because they want money and fame and the clout of being a listed company. The founder might well see a flotation as a crowning achievement in a successful career. The private equity backers may well see it as a chance to grab the money and run. They are all keen to see a high valuation. They therefore build expectations and share their hopes for growth among the investment community.

This incendiary mixture ignites passions among the investing public and perhaps even the financial media. Shares sold in an IPO can soar to a thrilling premium, as imaginations run riot over the future bounties the company will reap. Investors and the media jump over themselves to suggest ever more amazing sales and profits progress their new darling is destined to make. Its dynamism knows no bounds! The sky's the limit!

Meanwhile the management of the newly public company are seduced by all the attention and the glory. They are heroes who have made everyone money. Now they are really big shots down at the golf club. Confidence and expenses rise. So they need new hirings, new premises, new company cars – all befitting of such a visibly successful outfit. Very soon the acquisitions start, egged on by clever financial advisers, hungry for fees. The first deal might be safe enough, but quickly enthusiasm gets the better of judgement, and worse companies are bought. After all, much of the currency being used are highly-rated shares – and initially at least all the acquisitions are earnings-enhancing.

Behind the scenes all is not so buoyant. Rapid expansion has led to teething problems. The senior management have been distracted by the glamour of the City. Some of the quick-fire acquisitions have turned sour. The competition has learned what juicy margins the company enjoys, now all is clearly displayed in the accounts and broker's circulars, and are copying them. The customers are squeezing prices, having also learned about the impressive margins.

But the bandwagon rolls on. More analysts visit and write glowing notes, each outdoing the other to upgrade earnings estimates – and so boost expectations. The pressure on management to deliver hyper-growth is ever more intense – just as the market is slowing and business is getting tough. Now acquisitions are made to get the company out of trouble, and bury the profit shortfall. Unfortunately such deals rarely work, and bad companies are bought for too much money. They compound the difficulties.

The story starts to unravel. The able people leave. The founders try to cash out of their shares, knowing trouble is looming. The accounts get more and more cooked. Borrowings rise, because the shares start to slide and so the paper can no longer be used. Eventually the dreaded profit warning comes out and the whole caper is up. The whirlwind romance is over, and like bitter ex-lovers, the shareholders, analysts and media turn on the company and its management in disappointment, revenge and fury.

Recrimination and blame fly around and the shares crash and

further profit warnings come out. There are sackings and unfair dismissal claims. New non-executives are appointed and company doctors sent for. Numbers are restated and profits become huge losses. The bankers get scared and call in investigating accountants as covenants are breached. Gradually the business is dismembered, with sackings, shut subsidiaries and sell-offs.

The high-flyer is now a fallen angel, broken by an almost inexorable process whereby the City builds a company up so it can destroy it. This tale is so common as to be almost inevitable. The markets take sound companies and make too much of them. They get the management over-excited and force-feed them money. The ravenous beast devours its best offspring and regurgitates them in little pieces. I suppose this is the 'creative destruction' of capitalism in action.

December 1999

8

Business and Society

Who Says Tycoons Are Always Wicked?

Most writers have no first-hand experience of business; they often suspect that anyone who is successful in commerce is wicked. So they frequently portray entrepreneurs, tycoons and executives as grasping bullies, with hearts of stone and morals of a devil. Part of the problem is that everyday business can lack melodrama, so even talented authors find limited material to build great stories. The businessman as villain fits a classic stereotype which has been perpetuated in books, plays and films through the ages. This has tended to mean capitalism gets a poor showing in many memorable works of fiction, from Chaucer's smug merchant in *The Canterbury Tales* and the grasping Shylock in Shakespeare's *Merchant of Venice* onwards.

While Orson Welles' *Citizen Kane* may be regularly regarded as the best film of all time, Charles Foster Kane himself comes across as a frustrated egomaniac, and ultimately unhappy despite his wealth, power and success. Not very inspiring material for would-be builders of companies. Charles Dickens is invariably scathing about business, from his depiction of the proud and materialistic Mr Dombey in *Dombey & Son* to the sinister convict Magwitch in *Great Expectations*.

American writers have generally been better at making business seem real and exciting on the page, on screen and on the stage. This is probably because America has never adopted socialism as Europe has, and the Horatio Alger self-made man is part of their heritage. *Glengarry Glen Ross*, both a play and a film by David Mamet, is a searing description of a real-estate selling operation, and a brilliant dissection of the art of salesmanship. Richard Roma, played by Al Pacino in the film version, is the best salesman in the pack, and his ability to win over a complete stranger and close a sale is a superb piece of theatre and fairly true to life. Roma pitches his customer dreams rather than features and benefits – and that is why he buys. But overall the play reveals a grim, cut-throat world, and is hardly a job advert for the profession of estate agency. Together with Arthur Miller's classic play *Death of a Salesman*, the sad decline of Willy Loman, taken together they are enough to put anyone off a life in sales.

Jay Gatsby, the doomed subject of F. Scott Fitzgerald's marvellous book *The Great Gatsby*, is an example of a writer seeing a businessman as a fake and a crook. The tragic, charming bootlegger desperately tries to improve himself through illicitly-acquired wealth in order to win the beautiful Daisy, but it all turns to ashes. Too often, entrepreneurs in novels are characterised as ruthless criminals, rather like Jack Carter's bosses in Ted Lewis's book *Jack's Return Home*, which was made into Michael Caine's best film – *Get Carter*.

Showbiz impresarios do not fair well in fiction, be it the movies like *The Player*, Gene Wilder's *The Producers*, Fitzgerald's unfinished final novel *The Last Tycoon*, or Budd Schulberg's novel *What Makes Sammy Run?* The latter is a story set in Hollywood in the 1930s, the era of the great producers like Samuel Goldwyn and David O. Selznick. The Sammy of the title is Sammy Glick, a pushy and ruthless ghetto boy who claws his way up from the slums of New York to wild success as a Californian movie mogul, destroying all in his path. He adopted the philosophy of Spanish general Ramon Maria Navarez, who was asked when he was dying by a priest. "Does your Excellency forgive all of your enemies?" "I do not have to forgive my enemies," answered Navarez. "I have had them all shot."

Glick ends up king of all he surveys, but bewildered by his ambition. He is a recurrence of the Howard Hughes/Citizen Kane theme in fiction – vast riches, but little fulfilment. Perhaps the idea that untold wealth and power do not bring a contented life makes creators of fiction feel better about being bossed around by studios and publishers and not getting sufficient royalties!

Anthony Trollope is now recognised as one of the greatest of Victorian novelists. Unfortunately he too gave tycoons a hard time. His most devastating attack is in *The Way We Live Now*, the story of a giant fraud perpetrated by the financier Melmotte and his partners, who promote a grand trans-American railroad and steal the proceeds from gullible investors. Inevitably Melmotte overreaches himself and gets his just deserts. "Wonderful are the ways of trade," writes Trollope with irony.

Graham Greene, one of Britain's finest 20th century novelists, normally had it in for moguls. His excellent thriller *A Gun For Sale* features the nasty arms dealer Sir Marcus of Midland Steel, who orders executions and encourages wars. Even the seedy hitman Raven is a heroic figure compared to the grim avarice of Sir Marcus, who is eventually shot. It seems rich capitalists always make easily identifiable baddies – especially if they do things like manufacture munitions.

It is hard for aspiring entrepreneurs to gain inspiration from the depiction of business in most fictional works. Be it the awful banker in Frank Capra's *It's a Wonderful Life* or the maniac Gordon Gekko played by Michael Douglas in *Wall Street*, there are few positive role models. The scriptwriters, novelists and playwrights all seem to despise mercantile achievement. There is the occasional bright endorsement of business enterprise – Francis Ford Coppala's semi-fictional film *Tucker* about the automobile entrepreneur, or *Mildred Pierce*, a story by James M. Cain of a bold female entrepreneur. But these are the rare exceptions. It seems that if you are a rich capitalist in fiction, then you are sure to be a wrong 'un. We need more great books, films and drama with business builders as heroes.

March 2001

Public vs Private Sector

One of the great challenges facing society is how to balance the public and private sectors. Even the most ardent free market advocates acknowledge that some services – defence and the police, for example – are best delivered by the state. But equally, many citizens of all political persuasions accept that private enterprise tends to be more dynamic and efficient than government-controlled organisations. So what are the intrinsic differences between the way the public and private sectors function?

- In the private sector, the chief incentives are financial. In the public sector, staff are incentivised by goodwill and rules. The concepts of bonuses, performance-related pay, or share options are alien in the NHS, education sector or civil service. It offends all the traditionalists to even suggest such things – and would be hard to quantify anyway. But in a materialistic age, it becomes ever harder to motivate workers with intangibles alone: people want monetary rewards. The diminution in deference for many public workers like firemen, doctors, nurses, police, soldiers and teachers, and a decline in the sense of civic duty mean higher levels of demoralisation and absenteeism than in previous generations in the public sector.

- Measuring performance is easier in the private sector. It is measured by increased sales, or profits, or a higher share price, or a certain return on capital or cash generation. The criteria for success in the public sector are much more nebulous and open to debate and manipulation. Targets and assessments are part of modern government but their effectiveness is questionable. The very nature of what public servants do, such as fight wars, prevent crime, cure the sick, teach children, etc. means that results are not expressed in simple numerical terms.

- This all means that delegation and local empowerment within the public sector are difficult. Such methods of management demand flexibility and rewards linked directly to outcomes. I have never seen a multi-site retailer work without a decent branch manager bonus system. The best such managers treat the business as their own, within limits. Whereas the tendency within government is to centralise and defer decision-making upwards, since the punishment for failure is always greater than the benefits of success. Westminster's emasculation of local government confirms this predilection.

- Yet curiously, capitalism is mostly about individuals, not committees. The state machinery comprises giant bodies like the NHS or DoE or Ministry of Defence. By contrast, lone entrepreneurs or partners start and develop new firms, and a large proportion of jobs and wealth are generated by innovative smaller companies. Capitalism is about embracing risk and challenging the status quo: state organisations are by their nature risk-averse, and run by consensus. While individuals in the state sector can make a difference, at its heart is endless process, procedure, hierarchy and conformity. Ultimately, public sector bodies are mainly about protecting the downside, while the private sector is about aiming for an upside. This produces a different level of enthusiasm and applied innovation.

- Government departments are dominated by politics, ritual, qualifications, theory, spin and elections. Business is more obsessed by practical outcomes like numbers of products sold, margins achieved or market share lost. Politicians talk endlessly about green papers, white papers, speeches and votes: few talk about the actual achievements of specific educational, health, law and order or other initiatives.

- Normally state services are a monopoly and so do not have to compete for customers. Virtually all private sector industries are ferociously competitive and have to match rivals on price, quality, service and so forth. This conditioning forces improvement. Another private sector threat which ensures the survival of the fittest is bankruptcy, the fate of companies which cannot remain solvent. State bodies face no such sanction, and so there is less imperative for continuous progress and vigilance over costs.

Over a number of years I've worked with various state organisations in health, education and media. Those that embraced more habits of the private sector – performance bonuses, true local management, market disciplines and so forth – fared better. Unreconstructed, unionised state monopolies resist reform and fail to adapt to the changing requirements of the taxpayer. They tend to offer poor value and don't work.

February 2006

Public Schools

This week a depressing survey was published showing how the privately educated still dominate virtually every profession in this country. Yet only 7% of all pupils are taught at fee-paying schools. This unique and tragic feature of our society perpetuates inequality more than any other aspect of life in Britain in the 21st century.

As far as business goes, studies show that under a third of FTSE 100 Chief Executives went to private schools, whereas 76% of judges did, while even 56% of top journalists are public school educated. This reveals that even in the structured, institutional end of commerce, there is less of a bias towards the privately-educated than in many careers. And I would guess that among leaders of entrepreneurial firms, it is an even smaller proportion – perhaps less than 25% of true entrepreneurs are from independent schools. The reason is clear: qualifications mean little if you are building a company in the rough and tumble of the marketplace. Moreover risk-taking – indeed capitalism – is not something academia really encourages. No wonder the legal profession – always worried about the downside – is so utterly in the grip of the highly-educated, highly-privileged few.

However, one critical area of business life where the public schools have complete hegemony is the City. The ruling classes have traditionally held sway in the Square Mile, and the only change from that over recent decades has been the arrival of a global elite of bankers from places like America, Switzerland and Japan. Lloyds, a cornerstone of the City for centuries, has always been run by ex-public school boys. Even in newer, powerful sectors like private equity and hedge funds, among the British players the vast majority are public school educated.

Of course the financial services are generally meritocratic, in the sense that the really able and clever can get ahead and make fortunes, whatever their schooling – but only once they are in the club. To join investment banks, asset managers, management consultants, law and accountancy firms and the like you really need to be articulate, and have a tremendous academic track record. The other crucial ingredient is self-confidence and belief – and the major public schools specialise in giving their pupils plenty of that.

I went to a Grammar School, and regret their passing. They offered decent opportunities for those in the state sector, and almost a third of senior industrialists went to them. Over 90% of children now attend comprehensives, and the impression is that standards have been dumbed down in the transition from selective schooling. It seems Gresham's law has applied to education, and good schools have got worse, rather than bad schools improved. As in so many areas, the government does not appear to manage education well. It is not even about money or resources, since state educational spending has increased dramatically in recent years. It is about attitudes, policies and motivation. And since almost the entire elite of the country educate their children privately, how much do they really care about state schools?

All this superior schooling comes at a high price. I have often felt at a competitive advantage over would-be entrepreneurs who have children relatively young. They cannot afford to leave their well-paid jobs, because then they could not meet the £25,000 a year after-tax cost of the top boarding schools which their children attend! So they remain in comfy, salaried employment and do not break out and plunge into the world of running their own show. I have only become a father recently, at the age of 43. My wife went to a comprehensive but has two degrees and an MBA. Despite our misgivings and our schooling, I suspect we shall do the obvious when it comes to educating our children.

I believe money and background matter less if young people pursue a career in business than in fields like the media and politics, or professions like medicine and architecture – and that is unquestionably a good thing. Enterprise is all about social mobility, which is why so many ambitious immigrants are successful in business here. Unquestionably the huge spread of higher education – now approaching 40% attend a university of some kind – mean more graduates build companies. But even so, many business superstars, from Branson to Sugar to Dunstone – did not pursue a degree of any kind, and it doesn't seem to have done them any harm. Perhaps the independent spirit rebels against the formal nature of education. But even if posh schooling matters less to entrepreneurs, we should all work to reform our education system, which emphasises divisions and holds back talent.

June 2006

The Lawyers Will Kill Us All!

There is a movie currently showing called *Devil's Advocate* which stars Al Pacino playing the Devil. I recommend those lawyers with a sensitive disposition avoid it. Lucifer's earthly manifestation is as the Senior Partner in an all-powerful New York law firm. I enjoyed the film, especially in its portrayal of US attorneys as a prime source of wickedness. Indeed, I would say the scriptwriter got it right: in many respects American lawyers represent evil incarnate in the modern world.

Now that is a rather strong statement, but in America at least the legal system – fostered and fed by the lawyers – is choking society. It is gradually suffocating under mountains of legislation, court cases and lawyers. And in Britain we are, as ever, copying some of the worst habits of the New World. Already we have a Prime Ministerial couple of barristers to match Three Dollar Bill Clinton and Hillary. And Cherie Blair inevitably practises one of the more noxious new branches of the law – employment litigation.

Ask anyone who employs lots of people and creates jobs what one of their biggest growing headaches is and they will tell you – vexatious litigant employees jumping on the payout bandwagon, egged on by grasping lawyers and a flawed system. Senior staff at several of the firms I work with spend days locked in preposterous industrial tribunals dealing with fired staff bringing unfair dismissal claims because they were caught stealing or assaulting other staff or customers. Invariably, the dismissed staff tell huge lies and are believed. If they are from an ethnic minority they are always advised to suggest they suffered racial discrimination. The entire process is a great waste of time and serious discouragement to those who are our only hope of really tackling unemployment.

Thank God, Britain has a long way to go before it truly catches up with the legal madness that has gripped America in the last thirty years. While we have only 70,000 practising solicitors, by the year 2000 there will be one million lawyers in the United

States. These 'professionals' need to make a living of course, so they manufacture legal actions and lobby politicians to pass new laws. And since all too many politicians are lawyers, and members of the same club, they are only too happy to oblige. After all, one in ten inhabitants of the City of Washington DC is a lawyer. Indeed, the US has 70% of the world's lawyers: that is why there are 18 million new lawsuits launched in America every year. And while civil legal actions in the UK absorb around 0.7% of GNP, in the US the figure is almost 2.5%.

The medical profession is reaching near paralysis in certain US states thanks to malpractice lawsuits. For example, the way in which babies are born has been profoundly influenced: almost 25% of all US child births are by Caesarean section, the most invasive and expensive procedure, but also the form of birth least likely to get a doctor sued. It is no coincidence that rates of Caesarean births are much higher in the US than elsewhere. The medical profession there practises defensive medicine, not designed to protect the patient, but the surgeon!

Unfortunately, the public here read about huge compensation payments against the medical profession in the US, and fancy their chances. So insurance premiums for British health professionals are climbing steadily, and ever more of their time is spent filling in forms and worrying about being sued by patients. Ambulance chaser lawyers, willing to work on contingent payments, are eagerly promoting this tendency. All this will produce is more expensive medical treatment for all and a less caring medical profession – it will not make doctors better at their work.

Of course there are many fine, honourable lawyers who do a reputable job for fair recompense. But they are a shrinking number, as the greed factor and increasing competition corrupts and debases the high moral principles of legal practice. Increasingly, hours billed and fee rates charged have replaced any concerns about ethics or the contribution our lawyers make to society. Those who train to become lawyers and barristers should not do so for pure financial motives: they should seek to resolve problems rather than find them; they should not act for clients who lie; and they should not manipulate the system. Otherwise we will end up like the litigation swamp which America has become. In 1992 in Alabama a jury awarded $4 million in punitive damages to the owner of a new BMW against the car manufacturer because it had failed to disclose $601 worth of repainting – true madness!

January 2004

Twenty-First Century Philanthropists

The technology boom and the bull market have created unprecedented numbers of British millionaires. Even the number of self-made billionaires has tripled in the last five years. A lot of this wealth is in stock market paper, and not cash, but the rising individual prosperity of the 'new economy' rich is undeniable. Unlike many other waves of wealth, rather than institutions capturing the lion's share of the windfalls, companies such as Carphone Warehouse and Autonomy are showering their youthful founders with untold hundreds of millions.

So what are these new plutocrats going to do with their embarrassment of riches? They may well spend some on trinkets, like new boats, planes or country estates. They may well spoil their children and leave them vast inheritances. But those will not take effect for many decades. In the meantime, apart from investing in other business deals, I suspect there may be a big boost in corporate and personal philanthropy – and I think it will be a magnificent thing.

There are several reasons for this. First, Gordon Brown has helped charities and the taxpayer by creating some genuine tax incentives to encourage charitable giving. Taxpayers can now claim tax relief on both income and capital gains tax on charitable gifts.

Company owners can even transfer shares to a charity and claim tax relief on the asset. Legacies to charity are already exempt from inheritance tax. The Chancellor hopes these gestures will raise an extra £1bn for good causes by 2002. The Government has seen how the National Lottery has hit donations to charities and also seen how successful such tax breaks are in the US at encouraging the rich to give their money away.

Indeed, I think the super-rich in America have helped set an example which I believe our wealthy are following. Ted Turner's giant £1bn gift to the UN was just the most high-profile gesture of many generous acts by the US mega-rich. Both Warren Buffett and

Bill Gates have said they will leave the majority of their fortunes to charitable causes. Other, less well-known entrepreneurs are doing similar things.

There is a tidal wave of philanthropic cash, which will create enormous endowments and foundations for decades to come. This benevolence follows in a long tradition of giving, stemming from the earliest great robber baron capitalists such as Andrew Carnegie, the steel magnate, who constructed thousands of libraries and public buildings across Britain and America.

It is important that those who have done well materially give something back. It demonstrates that capitalists are not monsters, and do care about those less fortunate than themselves. Like community service and voluntary work, it binds people together. Government cannot provide everything – charities and non-profit organisations are a critical part of our civic life. And capitalists need to get involved in charity work to ensure that such organisations do not develop an anti-business agendas – which some of them are wont to do.

A recent book, *Bowling Alone: America's Declining Social Capital* by Robert Putnam, talks about the fragmentation of society thanks to the breakdown of traditional family structures and the rise of television and suchlike. Voluntary groups and community fundraising activities are almost the best way of combating such social alienation.

Working with disadvantaged groups brings the rich out of their limousines and high-walled mansions and gets them to mix with people from all walks of life. It helps counteract the uneven distribution of wealth that the 1990s boom has only amplified. It forces the ruling classes to stand in the bus queue rather than just stare at it through the mirrored glass of their stretch car.

The great thing is that there are thousands of fine causes and anyone with time and money to give can choose something personal to them where their efforts can make a real difference. The ways of raising money in the 21st century are endless, from charity shops to internet auctions to celebrity events to TV appeals.

Perhaps there are too many separate charities but the nature of giving is that it works best in small groups with passionate participants, rather than on a faceless, industrial scale with little personal connection. The structure of the charity world may be inefficient, but donors want to feel their contribution is important – in a world of just 25 charities this would not be possible.

I have always believed the best way to get bright well-off people to contribute to a cause is not just to ask for cash, but insist that they play a part in the whole process. That means they attend fund-raising events, sit on trust committees, make decisions on how money is spent and so forth.

Perhaps they are too busy to do these things, but most potential givers do not want to feel that it is just their loot that is attractive. They would like to think that their ideas and contacts are as useful as their bank accounts – and perhaps they are.

To reach the new generation of industrialists is not a pushover, but if they can be persuaded to copy their American counterparts, then perhaps we are about to enter a new, golden age of philanthropy.

July 2000

Reinventing the NHS

Until very recently I was involved with a major firm working with the NHS. I co-founded the business and spent ten years with it as a principal. This gave me an insight into the way we carry out healthcare in this country, and what reforms might be undertaken to get better value for the taxpayer from the roughly £92 billion annual NHS expenditure. This figure has risen from just £34 billion when Labour came to power, but only Patricia Hewitt thinks this is "the best year ever for the NHS".

Among initiatives I would undertake would be to:

- *Educate the taxpayer*
  If it is given away, demand for healthcare is almost infinite. The government should communicate to the public in blunt terms how resources are limited and explain that staff, buildings, drugs, and treatments are expensive. Through media briefings, online bulletins and other means the state must tell people that there will always be a degree of rationing. It is better to be honest than promise the impossible. Our expectations for perfection must be tempered.

- *Price everything properly*
  Every NHS treatment should be properly priced – from a GP appointment to a major operation – and the patient should be given a bill. This would not be paid in cash at the time, but it would let recipients know how much they were costing the system, would discourage waste and would make people appreciate the care they receive more.

- *Use paramedicals*
  The NHS is mainly staffed by highly-qualified professionals like doctors, nurses, dentists, pharmacists and so forth who are 'unionised' members of professional bodies like the BMA. These trade organisations have mostly done a terrific job on behalf of their members on pay in recent years. Wages have soared by huge amounts in many cases. These ill-advised

agreements cannot now be reversed, because the British never accept pay cuts. But more work could be farmed out to part-qualified individuals who would cost much less.

- *Reinvent the pension scheme*
  The current NHS Pension Scheme is economically unsustainable and should be closed. The terms and benefits for members should be substantially revised. Given the huge pay increases of recent times, the future burden of the current final salary scheme is sure to lead to crisis unless things change. Medical workers should face reality like those in the private sector.

- *Introduce incentive payments*
  Staff should be paid according to performance, as happens in most other walks of life. Bonuses should be given for those who actually deliver – nothing for those who fail.

- *Make private health costs tax-deductible*
  This will encourage those who can afford it to go private, and take pressure off the NHS. It will help encourage growth in private care, so providing competition to the NHS and forcing it to improve.

- *Do regional pay deals*
  Staff should not earn the same in different parts of the country where living costs vary dramatically. Rates of pay should reflect local accommodation and other expenses.

- *Change the law on medical negligence*
  Growth in the numbers and size of claims are undermining morale, wasting resources and costing the taxpayer too much. The legal profession should be prevented from exploiting the state.

- *Scrap Connecting for Health, the NHS IT scheme*
  This mega-programme may end up costing £30 billion or more. It is wildly over-ambitious and bound to fail, like so many huge computer projects carried out by government.

- *Let doctors and nurses manage*
  These are highly intelligent, educated people, who understand clinical issues better than the bureaucrats ever will. They should be taught the economics of healthcare and encouraged to run their own organisations – the politicians should keep out.

- *Introduce stricter NHS registers*
  As voters must be on the electoral roll, so patients who want treatment must prove they are qualifying citizens – to prevent 'health tourists' who come here to take advantage of our system.

- *Manage locally but buy nationally*
  Wherever possible, hospitals, surgeries, clinics and other facilities should control their own destinies, to give staff a sense of ownership and loyalty. But purchasing of drugs and other supplies should continue on a UK basis to exploit economies of scale.

- *Exclude 'lifestyle' treatments*
  The NHS should not carry out cosmetic surgery, sex-change operations or IVF treatments, or prescribe drugs like Viagra. Patients should take out insurance or fund such treatments themselves.

Ultimately an organisation of 1.3 million employees is unmanageable. We should realise that the Bevanite model of 1948 no longer works, and introduce an insurance-based scheme and limit the state's involvement to basic healthcare only. But citizens will take some time to be persuaded to give up their emotional attachment to the old NHS and adopt a healthcare model fit for the 21st century.

June 2006

Money War of the Ages

Historically the principal battles for the control and distribution of wealth were fought between countries, empires, and competing merchants. In the future, I suspect the war could be between the generations within each society.

Essentially the old have all the capital, and the young want to possess it. As people age, they accumulate assets both through work and inheritance, but they also tend to become more risk-averse – perhaps because they have more to lose. Over time the average lifespan has increased and we have become more prosperous, so more wealth has accumulated among the elderly. The rise of occupational pensions and the tax breaks they enjoy have compounded this enrichment enormously.

Many pension holders in middle age do not realise that their largest asset is not their home but their pension and life policies. The decline of traditional family values and religion have exaggerated the divisions between the age groups, since the breaking of communal ties from previous eras has fragmented families. The vast inflation of property values in Britain in the last 50 years means thanks to inheritance the late middle-aged are now becoming the richest generation of all time.

This is all very well, but for society to advance assets must turn over and be put to productive use. Over-careful hoarding of wealth will not increase our standard of living and would be doing a disservice to future generations. Britain's well developed stock market and our cult of equity has directed money towards entrepreneurs who can use it. Professional money managers are all ages and help decide the allocation of capital. I suspect the best institutional investment houses are those with a proper weighting of age and youth, experience tempered with a touch of youthful flair.

All advanced nations have ageing populations. With adequate lifetime pension provision and restrained expenditure on healthcare, we can afford to cope with this shift in demographics while maintaining living standards. But pressures can grow where dwindling numbers of younger workers must pay for rising numbers of pensions out of current taxes. Several Continental European nations may face the problem of inter-generational resentments in the coming decades.

Youth of course is intoxicated with risk, change and technology. These drive economic progress in society, but they are alien to many in the older generation. Investment capital is owned by the old, who want security and income, rather than to gamble on wild new ideas and the unknown. The old see solid values disappearing and reckless behaviour taking hold. Youngsters see opportunities denied because of lack of imagination and over-caution among their elders.

The largest single force which has driven commerce through the ages is technology. This is the territory of youth. Our seniors must temper the leading edge stuff to make it safe and useful. Working together is likely to deliver the best results. Bankers must adopt characteristics of both youth and age when making lending decisions. If we play too safe, we risk relentless impoverishment; if we are too bold, we risk a South Korean type meltdown. Innovators are needed, but alongside them should be sages who remember previous recessions and crashes.

In many respects society's most wasted asset is not the unemployed young, but the underemployed old. Those of 60 and older are frequently retired – and many do-gooders would have us reduce the age of retirement further. Veterans are meant to relax, have holidays, do the garden and enjoy life. Yet how much energy and experience and knowledge there is among that group! Many of the wisest and funniest people in business I've met have been over 60. They possess far more patience than I do and have seen so much before.

The best among the elderly do not cling to power and assets. They involve the younger generations and work with them. They enjoy their company and make an effort to understand their enthusiasms. After all, age is really a state of mind.

I have been privileged to serve on several company boards with non-executives in their sixties and seventies, and in most cases they have been huge contributors. They tend to have time and take trouble. They have less impetuous ambition and a more balanced view. Frequently they have superb contacts built up over a lifetime of networking. And the best ones welcome as partners young capitalists in their twenties and thirties with grand visions but much to learn.

There are inevitably barriers to overcome. Youth must not dismiss people because they are as old as their grandparents. The elderly must actively seek out young associates and humour their exuberance. The combination of skills and outlooks is a powerful force which can help us better adapt and compete economically. After all, the 'grey' market is a huge new area which will continue expanding as people live longer and retire rich. The young need to help the old, listen to them and study them. We need some sort of national business network to bring together the wisdom and grey hairs of experienced retired business-types with the young go-getters who are the nation's future.

The most visible example of the conflicts of the ages is in Russia, where those under 40 believe in free enterprise, want to copy the West and want to get rich – by whatever means is necessary. The older generations long for the certainties of communism, when there was less flash, Russia was a proud empire, and workers got paid whether the work they did was purposeful or not. The new system is better, but takes getting used to: the young are adapting while the old find it painful. That is why Russia has more billionaires under 40 than anywhere else. Overall, I am not convinced that is altogether a good thing. Better perhaps to have an even spread of riches between the young chancers and the old wiseacres. That way they can teach each other lessons.

September 2002

Appendix

A list of books referred to in the articles

To read more about and buy any of these books, visit:

www.lukejohnson.org